As I read this wonderful, authentic manuscript by Marian Rizzo, I hummed "I walked today where Jesus walked and felt His presence there;" I was visually with Jesus. My grandson, Spencer, and I visited Israel in January 2000, and this book would have helped us feel His presence had we read it then.

Marian and I share newspaper writing backgrounds and our love for Jesus; her talent for the perfect ideas, descriptive words, and phrases that make you a part of her stories is inspired from Above. I felt I was *In The Boat With Jesus!*

~Paul Ferguson
retired reporter/editor/author/commercial printer.

As you read the Bible, you experience places and events in an academic way; you can't see the sunsets, quiet places of prayer on the mountains or busy throngs in marketplaces. When you visit Israel, you experience the Scriptures in a whole new way.

My wife, Cathy and I, visited the Holy Land. We were on the Sea of Galilee tourist boat, similar to fishing boats of *In The Boat With Jesus*, Marian Rizzo's new book. It was sunny and bright; winds were calm, and birds were sailing along without a care; the shoreline looks much as in the time of Jesus. Suddenly, the sky darkened, the wind picked up, the birds disappeared, and we were in a true maelstrom. The boat began to toss and pitch, and we realized how quickly meteorological events arose in the time of Jesus.

It was scary, just as Ms. Rizzo presents a virtual experience of the disciples in her book, and I could see them doing everything they could to save the boat—and there is Jesus, sleeping in the back. One word from Him and the storm ceased, and all was well. Nothing like a personal experience to shed light on an academic situation.

In her book, Ms. Rizzo brings you alive in Jesus' ministry, His crucifixion, resurrection, and ascension to His Heavenly throne.

~The Rev. Donald J. Curran, U.S. Navy Commander, Retired
Rector at Christ the King Anglican Church of Ocala, Florida

Marian Rizzo breathes new life into this age-old Christmas carol. By weaving Bible culture and history with modern day examples, she gives the reader a deeper understanding of the meaning behind the lyrics. Each verse of the song becomes a powerful devotional message that inspires us to remember "the reason for the season." This is not a book you'll read once and lay aside; rather, it will become a traditional favorite that you'll reread each December to mark off the days until Christmas.

~Doris Hoover, award-winning author of
Quiet Moments in The Villages, A Treasure Hunt Devotional

As you read Marian Rizzo's *O Holy Night*, and experience the depth of meaning in the words of the famous Christmas song, you will be drawn closer to Jesus and His love for you. So, brew a cup of tea, grab a comfy chair, and enjoy this inspirational treasure.

~Delores Kight, award-winning writer and co-author
of the children's picture book, *Manny the Lamb*.

What a great book for fans of the song *O Holy Night*. Marian Rizzo not only talks about the concepts found in each line of the song, but she makes it into a devotional by connecting the concepts with the scripture itself. In addition to that, she is a gifted story-teller. I was touched in a way I wouldn't have suspected by very brief stories about a flight attendant named Hope and the account of a cat and a dog playing with each other. And all of this is woven together into a beautiful Christmas gift. I recommend it.

~Mario Villella, pastor of Good News Church Ocala
author of the booklet, *Working Our Way Through Life*

In the Boat with Jesus

Also by Marian Rizzo

The Legacy of Mrs. Cunningham
Silver Springs: The Liquid Heart of Florida
Angela's Treasures
Muldovah
In Search of The Beloved
In Search of Felicity
Plague
The Leper
Presence in the Pew
O Holy Night

In the B*oat* with *Jesus*

and other places where the savior walked
a virtual experience

MARIAN RIZZO

WordCrafts Press

*This book is dedicated to those missionaries
who go into all the world and preach the Gospel*

*With Special Thoughts of:
Andy and Chrissy Shaub serving in Ecuador
Bill and Katie Streeter, serving in Papua New Guinea
Tom and Lorie Leger, who have served in multiple places in the world*

THE AGE-LONG MINUTE
by *Amy Carmichael*

Thou art the Lord who slept upon the pillow;
Thou art the Lord who soothed the furious sea;
What matter beating wind and tossing billow
If only we are in the boat with Thee?

Hold us in quiet through the age-long minute
While Thou art silent, and the wind is shrill.
Can the boat sink while Thou, dear Lord, art in it?
Can the heart faint that waiteth on They will?

Contents

Wouldn't it be nice to spend real time with Jesus? To walk beside Him on the road to Emmaus? To stroll with Him on the shores of Galilee? To open Martha's front door and find Him standing there?

Tap into your imagination. Envision the people Jesus met. Inhale the salty breeze off the lake. Turn your ear toward the bleat of the lamb and the coo of the dove. Lean against a rock wall and watch Him mingle with the lowly. Dine with Him in the upper room. Pray with Him on Gethsemane. Bow before His cross. Enter His empty tomb.

Israel is unfamiliar territory to many people. Few have tread upon the rocky wilderness of Judea or dipped their toes in the Jordan. Few have witnessed the sun rising behind the mountains of Moab or plucked an olive from a gnarled tree in the garden. Few have camped out under the star-filled sky that spread its arms of welcome to angels on that holy night more than 2,000 years ago.

Travel now beyond the pages of this book into the very presence of Jesus. Rub elbows with Simon Peter, place your head beside John's on the Savior's breast. Join the crowd as they lay their cloaks and palm branches before Him. Dine with Him in the home of Martha and Mary. Weep with Him at the tomb of Lazarus. Then rise up in anger at the Lord's trial and crucifixion. Mourn with His followers, celebrate His resurrection, stand on the Mount of Olives as He ascends into heaven, and witness Him in His glory.

Let the lessons He taught 2,000 years ago help you deal with today's issues. Learn from Him. Apply His teachings. And make His story *your* story.

Chapter One

IN THE STABLE WITH JESUS
Making Room for the Savior

Reading: Luke 2:1-20

It's the first century AD. An innkeeper in Bethlehem has filled his hostel with visitors. Now he keeps repeating the words, "Sorry, no room."

"No room," he says to the stragglers who are pouring into the little town. "No room," to a young Galilean couple who come knocking on his door.

All of the inns in Judea are overflowing with people who have come there to register and pay taxes, as ordered by Caesar Augustus. It's also the Passover, as evidenced by the steady stream of black smoke rising from the temple. Shepherds make regular trips into Jerusalem where they sell their unblemished lambs in the market-place or present the finest of their flocks as offerings to be sacrificed by the temple priests.

Now, you've joined up with a group of those shepherds. They've left their herds grazing in a nearby pasture. They say they are responding to a miraculous summons they witnessed only last night in the field. Instead of hauling more lambs to the Holy City, they're going instead to the little town of Bethlehem. Their faces are aglow with passion. Their voices sing about a heavenly vision involving a bright light, angels, and a message that the awaited Messiah has at last come to Judea.

You're caught up in their passion. The Messiah? Your heartbeat quickens. You've also been awaiting His arrival. You've read the scriptures. You know the prophecies. You can barely contain your excitement.

You try to keep up with the shepherds as they rush ahead of you. The smell of sheep dung rises from their sandals. Their cloaks appear tattered from years of hard labor. Their callused hands grip roughly-carved staffs. They're a dirty, unkempt bunch. But you stay with them, eager to see the prophecy come to fruition.

The way is rough. Sharp rocks, gullies, and mounds of brittle grass litter the path. A stone lodges in your sandal, and you stop to pluck it out. The balmy night air paints beads of perspiration on your brow. One of the shepherds wraps a scarf around your forehead to stem the flow. Your feet ache from stumbling over the uneven ground. Nevertheless, you struggle on.

Suddenly, a shout of exaltation goes up near the front of the pack. Ahead lies Bethlehem, the "House of Bread," with its clay dwellings and flat-topped roofs. Tents have been erected on the hill. Campfires illuminate the limestone ridge. Plumes of smoke give off a hint of cedar mixed with animal feces. Shrouded figures hunch in half-circles around the fires, their voices rising in muffled discourse. As you pass, their heads briefly turn in your direction.

The shepherds ignore the people at the campfires and hurry past them. They've located the stable, a mere cave carved out of the limestone ridge. It's nothing more than a filthy refuge for beasts of burden. Above the cave a lighted inn swells with the loud voices of raucous guests. But your eyes are on the cave below.

A flicker of light beckons you to the open door. The shepherds enter first. Holding your breath, you step cautiously inside and are immediately struck by the scent of fresh hay and sweet mashed corn, evidence that animals recently found shelter there. But there are no donkeys or goats in this place tonight. The floor has been swept clean. In the center of the cave a man and a woman peer back at you with dark, welcoming eyes. He's wearing a woolen tunic, a sleeveless robe woven from goat's hair, and thick leather sandals on his feet. She's reclining on the ground, her weary form concealed within a swath of veils. Between them is a stone trough, commonly used to feed the animals.

You look around the close quarters, but see no sign of royalty. No clue that the Messiah has arrived. Confused, you draw closer to the trough and peer over the edge. Inside lies a newborn babe, swaddled in strips of linen. No crown graces His head. His tiny hand holds no scepter. Yet, a lump comes to your throat. Your eyes sting with tears as a blessed realization strikes your heart.

The child's swathing bears a stark resemblance to the wrappings at a person's burial—linen strips wound tightly from head to toe, with only a small opening at the face where a napkin would be placed during the final ritual. But this is a child, not a corpse. It's a newborn babe, ready for life, not the grave.

If this truly is the Messiah, then why didn't the owner of the inn offer lodging? Anger burns within you. No room in the inn? Not even for the Messiah?

Then a bitter truth penetrates your soul. When have *you* made room for Him? When have you taken time in your busy schedule to pause for a moment of prayer? When did you last include Him in your decisions? When did you last speak of Him to others?

Don't be like the innkeeper who relegated the holy family to a dirty cave beneath his hotel. Make room for the Savior.

Behold, I stand at the door and knock. If anyone hears My voice and opens the door, I will come in to him and dine with him, and He with Me.

~Revelation 3:20

Chapter Two

IN THE HOUSE WITH JESUS
The Act of Giving

Reading: Matthew 2:1-12

Two years after you visited the stable with a band of lowly shepherds, you're now riding on a camel, and your companions are royalty from afar. They're wearing elegant robes woven from silk and embellished with threads of brilliant colors. Their bright raiment sets off the deep brown of their skin. Jeweled turbans crown their heads, and brilliant gemstones adorn their fingers and toes.

They hail from the east—astrologers, they claim, who have studied the stars—wise men, who insist the prophecies have been fulfilled. They turn their eyes toward the heavens and concentrate on a light of great size moving slowly toward the west.

A discussion arises among them. Could the bright light be a conjunction of Jupiter and Saturn? Or possibly it came from a terrible explosion in the heavens. Or, some attest, an all-powerful God created the phenomenon for this very moment. You ponder their suggestions and ride on, your camel plodding along, the rhythmic clop of his hooves keeping time with the jingle of bells on his harness.

The dry desert air has left you with parched lips. You're grateful when the travelers pause beside a stream. Like the others, you dismount and allow your camel to lap up the refreshing liquid. You remove the goatskin flask from your shoulder, uncap it, and gulp down the sweet, refreshing milk. Then you fill the empty container with water.

Immediately, the leader of the group shouts a command. You clamber onto your camel. The beast rises from the ground, back end first, nearly causing you to topple from the saddle. You grip the horn and remain steady as his front end shifts upward. Then, emitting a loud snort, your animal falls in step with the others. A cacophony of jingling harnesses and stomping animal hooves fills the air as the riders fall in line once again.

According to the leader, the journey has taken several days. They enter the Holy City and progress uphill toward the palace of King Herod himself.

Your heart trembles with fear for the magi, for you've heard stories about the vicious, unpredictable Idumaean ruler. It's been said he murders people who offend him, even members of his own family.

You wait outside and pray for those travelers who are venturing into the palace. Sometime later, they emerge, unharmed, to your relief. With little explanation, they lead the caravan out of the city, then down the hillside and along the valley to the town of Bethlehem. The village has changed little in the two years since you visited the stable. Just as before, flat-roofed, clay homes cluster together on the limestone ridge. Below the dwellings are the rock-hewn caves that serve as shelters for livestock. You're reminded of your last visit and experience a feeling of nostalgia as you pass the stable where Jesus was born. Except for a lonely donkey, the cave is empty now.

Throughout the journey, the magi have kept their attention on the bright light in the sky. Now it's come to rest above a simple, mud-built home, much like all the others on the ridge. There's one door, built so low you have to stoop a little to enter.

The boy's parents have changed little since you met them. They still have that welcoming sparkle in their dark eyes. The child, about two years old now, stands in front of His mother, His eyes intent on the visitors.

One by one, the magi step forward and lay their presents at the child's feet. One visitor unlaces the strings on a velvet pouch. Pieces of gold spill out and scatter like a noisy waterfall on the tile floor. Another uncaps a ceramic bottle and releases the musky sting of frankincense into the air. Still another breaks an alabaster jar which emits the warm essence of myrrh.

Again, you're startled with a profound revelation. Just as the babe's swaddling clothes were reminiscent of burial wrappings, these aromatic offerings also bring to mind the embalming fluids the Jewish people typically use to anoint their deceased.

You watch in awe as more gifts are placed before the child, and you wonder, what can you give that would compare with such treasures? You check your pockets. Empty. Your purse. Nothing of value in there. Ashamed, you begin to turn away.

Then you stop, aware that you already possess the gift He is seeking. Though you may rightfully be willing to give of your wealth, your hopes, and your dreams, what He really wants is *yourself.* Not merely as a gift to God, but to others in God's name. When you give yourself to Him, it opens the door to give yourself to others. And when you give anything to others, you're bringing great pleasure to Him.

So let each one give as he purposes in his heart, not grudgingly or of necessity: for God loves a cheerful giver.

~2 Corinthians 9:7

Chapter Three

IN NAZARETH WITH JESUS
The Father's Business

Reading: Luke 2:40-52

Eager to catch a glimpse of Jesus during His youth, you travel to Nazareth, a small village nestled in the foothills on the southwest side of the Sea of Galilee. There, you locate the home of Mary, His mother, and Joseph, Jesus' stepfather. Their dwelling lies amidst a cluster of similar sand-colored, mud-brick houses grouped together on the porous rock twelve miles from the sea.

Jesus is now twelve years old. While Bethlehem, the place of His birth, fulfilled the prophet Micah's prediction that the ruler of Israel would come out of that little town in Judea, the village of Nazareth has embraced Him during the early years of His life.

As you weave along the narrow streets you pass several cisterns and a community well where the residents get their water. High on a hill stands the town's synagogue, where Sabbath services are observed and where young boys go during the week to learn to read and write and to study the Torah. The glistening stone construction resembles a giant mirror with its broad front reflecting the glare of the sun onto the houses below.

The population of about 400 consists of hard-working laborers, mostly farmers and tradesmen. Among them is this humble carpenter named Joseph. You've come purposely to this home, eager to see how Mary's firstborn son has fared.

Just before reaching the front door you pass Joseph's workshop, a narrow shelter carved out of the limestone ridge. A wooden bench stands at the far end where tools are neatly stored and arranged. They're simple tools—chisels, saws, mallets, an adz, and a bow drill—all of them cleaned to a shine, sharpened, and ready for use. On the floor against the wall stand several uncompleted projects.

A cart wheel, a yoke for oxen, door frames, and handles for rakes and hoes. Outside is a stack of hewn lumber ready for the next customer's need.

You approach the front door. The opening is hardly taller than you are. Your heart beats with anticipation as you move from blinding sunlight into a cool interior. A tile floor glistens beneath an open window, and the furnishings seem humble but adequate.

You're greeted by familiar pairs of welcoming eyes and out-stretched hands that momentarily take you back more than a decade to Bethlehem. A lump of nostalgia rises to your throat. You accept an invitation to sit at the table where a midday meal has been set out. A platter of raisin cakes, fresh from the hearth, slices of freshly seared lamb, and cups of herbal tea.

Joseph blesses the food, then you bite into a cake and relish the sweet taste of raisins and honey. While sipping tea from a ceramic cup you look around the table at the gathering. Jesus is sitting beside His mother. It appears that other children have joined the household since the family returned to their hometown. Mary's firstborn Son now has younger brothers and sisters. James is next in age, and Joses is yet a small child. Mary, who seems to be eternally pregnant these days, is considering Joseph's suggestions of names for future sons. Simon and Jude are two favorites. And, they mention various female names if their next child happens to be a daughter.

Their conversation turns to a discussion regarding their last visit to Jerusalem, when they went there for Passover, as is their habit from year-to-year.

"Jesus tarried behind," says Joseph, shaking his head in frustration. "We had traveled an entire day toward home when we discovered He wasn't with our party."

Then Mary tells of their tedious return to Jerusalem and their search for Jesus. They finally located Him in the temple surrounded by the most educated men of the city. Though it is customary for the religious leaders to gather on the temple terrace and debate matters of the Law, Mary admits she was astonished that those learned men appeared to be impressed by Jesus' wealth of knowl-edge. She also confesses that she behaved as any other mother would and questioned Jesus about separating from the group to linger behind.

Her Son's answer puzzled her. "Why did you seek me? Did you not know that I must be about My Father's business?"

My Father's business. The phrase sounds odd coming from a young boy. If He'd been about His Father's business, He would be working in a carpenter shop with Joseph, wouldn't He?

But no. Jesus had come to earth from heaven. His Father's business was of a celestial nature. He'd been sent here to seek and to save the lost.

If that's the Father's business, shouldn't we also be involved? Shouldn't we be laborers in the field, planting the seeds, watering the plants, reaping the harvest? The Father had a job for Jesus, and He has a job for anyone who believes in His Son and is willing to obey the call. In that case, isn't the Father's business your responsibility, too?

Therefore, my brethren, be steadfast, immovable, always abounding in the work of the Lord, knowing that your labor is not in vain in the Lord.

~1 Corinthians 15:58

Chapter Four

AT THE RIVER JORDAN WITH JESUS
Professing Your Faith

Reading: Matthew 3:1-17

It's early in the day. You're standing on the banks of the River Jordan, not far from the town of Jericho. A strange, wild man has come out of the wilderness and has drawn a large crowd to the river.

You eye him with amusement. He's wearing a garment made from coarse camel's hair, with a leather girdle around his waist. His thick hair falls in matted tangles to his shoulders. His straggly beard trails to his chest.

Someone says his name is John, the son of an aged temple priest, Zachariah by name. With mounting fervor, he calls for repentance. His resounding voice draws you closer to the river where people from all parts of Judea have gathered.

You perch on a grassy knoll and peer out at the winding river as it rushes toward the Dead Sea. In some places the depth is nearly twelve feet. The flow tumbles over rocks and leaves swirling whirlpools behind, then rushes impatiently past the opposite shore. Closer to this side, the water has come to rest in an alcove where the Baptizer is standing knee-deep in a large pool. With a sweep of his hand, he beckons the throng closer.

"Repent," he shouts with much vigor, "for the kingdom of heaven is at hand!"

A human cascade tumbles down the knoll into the water. You stand to get a better view over the shoulders and heads of onlookers. A woman rushes past you and bumps your arm, causing you to stumble. You regain your footing, then, aware of a disturbance on the hill behind you, you turn to see a huddle of men in elegant robes and with black-and-white shawls flung over their shoulders.

They cross their arms and glare at the Baptizer, their eyes aflame, their mouths moving in silent curses.

Undaunted, John frowns back at them. "Brood of Vipers!" he boldly cries out. "Who warned you to flee from the wrath to come?"

You chuckle softly at his unhampered display of courage.

The men on the hill can do little with so many zealous people surrounding the Baptizer. In an effort to entrap him, they resort to challenging questions about who he is. Elijah? The Christ? If not, then who?

He merely claims to be "one who is crying in the wilderness," a harbinger of someone who is mightier and will come after him, whose shoes he insists he is not worthy to unloose.

Suddenly a lone figure emerges from the shadows. A hush falls over the crowd. In a booming voice, John points at the man. "Behold the Lamb of God who takes away the sins of the world."

Lamb of God? But this is Jesus, John's cousin, someone says. Their mothers are related. John is a mere six months older. Now he is baptizing, and Jesus has come there to be baptized. John shakes his head and again claims he is unworthy of such an honor. But Jesus persists, and declares He is there to fulfill all righteousness. He moves down the bank and steps closer to John.

They stand in the water, face-to-face—a barbarian of the wilderness and God in human form. Though Jesus is sinless and has no need of repentance or baptism, He is setting an example for others to follow.

As He rises from the river, the clouds overhead drift apart. A breath of vapor descends from the sky, flutters like the wings of a dove, and comes to rest on Jesus' head. Then, an audible voice declares, "This is My beloved Son, in whom I am well pleased."

You stand frozen. You have just witnessed the baptism of the Son of God.

Jesus leaves the riverbank and passes close to you. Droplets fall from His beard and splash against your cheek. You touch your hand to the moisture, but you don't brush it away. Instead, you shut your eyes and press the treasured drops against your skin.

Your momentary reverie is interrupted by John's booming voice as he continues to call the multitude into the river. People trickle down the hillside. Ignoring the religious officials, the Baptizer continues to immerse one person after another.

His robed adversaries spin away. With their rich cloaks fluttering behind them, they stride in a swell of arrogance back to the city.

The people ignore the interruption. They continue to spill like a human waterfall into the pool. One after another, John lowers them into the water. They raise up, their faces aglow, their mouths singing praises to God.

It's time for you to join the others. If you've not yet publicly professed your faith through baptism, you can still do so. You don't have to travel to the Middle East, although being baptized in the Jordan surely is a memorable experience. At your disposal are lakes and rivers, church fonts, and even swimming pools. But the location and the act itself aren't as important as what is happening in your heart. That is where true repentance and baptism take place.

And now why are you waiting? Arise and be baptized, and wash away your sins, calling on the name of the Lord.

~Acts 22:16

Chapter Five

IN THE WILDERNESS WITH JESUS
Fighting Temptation

Reading: Matthew 4:1-11

You're standing on the edge of the Judean wilderness, a coppery brown expanse that stretches all the way down to the Dead Sea. You shade your eyes against the piercing rays of the rising sun and scan the scene. Rocks of all sizes litter the desert. Dried up riverbeds and deep ravines cut into the landscape. Occasionally, an oasis appears in the distance, a mere strip of green against the stark wasteland. To the northeast the mauve-colored mountains of Moab stretch across the horizon like a protective barrier against invaders. But for now, the desert is at rest.

Taking a deep breath, you venture down the limestone hillside and step precariously onto the stony trail. You were told Jesus left the city immediately after His baptism and was driven into the wilderness by the Spirit of God. He's been fasting there for forty days and forty nights.

When you find Him, you consider offering Him a piece of unleavened bread and a drink of water. But before you can draw close to Him, a shadow falls across the path. A chill passes through your body. You hold your breath, aware that the tempter has come.

Shamelessly, the devil challenges the Lord to a battle of wits. First, knowing Jesus has been fasting for forty days and nights, he dares the Lord to prove He is the Son of God by turning stones into bread. You look around at the rubble, aware that the Lord of all the earth created it all and can satisfy His hunger with a simple command.

But Jesus doesn't falter. He responds by quoting Deuteronomy 8:3, saying, *"It is written, 'Man shall not live by bread alone, but by every word that proceeds from the mouth of God.'"*

Then the tempter takes Him to a pinnacle of the temple. Anxious to meet them there, you race back to the city and enter the temple complex. The priests are padding about in bare feet. You slip out of your dirty sandals and mount the outer stair to the pinnacle, the highest point of the temple. It stands more than 200 feet above the southeast corner of the city. Your feet slide easily over the cool, uneven stones.

You arrive at the top just as Satan is putting forth his next challenge. The devil then dares Jesus to throw Himself off the pinnacle, trusting the angels to bear Him up. The place where Jesus stands is 450 feet above the Kidron Valley. Such a fall would mean certain death to an ordinary man. But Jesus is no ordinary man. In response to the devil's challenge, He once again quotes scripture, this time from Deuteronomy 6:16. *"It is written again, 'You shall not tempt the Lord your God.'"*

The devil then ushers Jesus to a high mountain. Exhausted from all the running around you've done, you hire a camel to take you to Mount Quarantania, a burnished summit in the Judean wilderness this side of Jericho. Your camel is fleet of foot. Minutes later, you arrive at the base of the mountain and weave through palm trees and lush vegetation. From there, your surefooted animal follows a winding trail to the top.

You look with awe at the panoramic view of Judea. Jerusalem looms on another high mountain in the west. You turn eastward and find Jericho and its flourishing valley, then in the far south, the deceptively deep blue color of the Dead Sea. The landscape ripples and changes, from lush vegetation and tall palm trees by the River Jordan to a parched wilderness, then the fruitful Mount of Olives and the great wall spanning the Holy City. Then you focus on the Lord and his adversary, close by on the mountaintop.

Satan is taking Jesus on a virtual tour of the kingdoms of the world and is promising to give it all to Him if He will bow down and worship him. You chuckle. The Lord already owns it all. Satan thought he could tempt Jesus with the lust of the flesh, the lust of the eyes, and the pride of life. It seems the deceiver has deceived himself.

Jesus again quotes scripture, from Deuteronomy 10:20. *"Away with you, Satan! For it is written, 'You shall worship the Lord your God, and Him only shall you serve.'"*

Defeated, Satan departs, and angels descend from heaven and minister to Jesus. As a human, He experienced the same weaknesses we also endure, but as God, He overcame them. Consider the series of events that occurred. Immediately after Jesus was baptized, Satan showed up to challenge Him. Preachers often warn people that after being publicly baptized persecution might come.

Think back to your own profession of faith and your baptism. What kind of persecutions did you face? Though Satan cannot take away your salvation, he can attempt to destroy your testimony. He can tempt you and bring failure or discouragement.

Jesus set an example for us. He countered the tempter's attacks with scripture. You can do the same, not only after baptism, but at any time during your Christian walk. You only need to arm yourself with the sword of the Spirit—Bible verses. Determine to memorize them. They will surely come to mind when you need them most.

Your word I have hid in my heart, That I might not sin against You.

~Psalm 119:11

Chapter Six

BY THE SEA OF GALILEE WITH JESUS
Fishing for Men

Reading: Mark 1:16-20

It's dawn. A sliver of daylight has begun to peer over the distant Golan Heights, more than seven miles away beyond the opposite shore of the Sea of Galilee. Moments later, the rippling hills form a purple shadow against the halo of light created by the rising sun. Soon the towns of Galilee will awaken to the merchants shouting out prices, the fishermen scaling their fresh-caught fish, and the tax collectors sorting coins on their tables in the center of town.

Since their youth, the local fishermen have worked in their families' business, a profitable career in this part of Israel. They live in well-built, nicely furnished homes. They stand out among the more respected men of the seaside villages. They are respected, trusted, and favored among the elite.

Simon Peter and Andrew are crouching by the water, immersing their nets in the sloshing tide, freeing them of seaweed and debris. They are not alone. Their partners, James and John, also are at work cleaning and mending their nets a short distance down the shoreline.

You venture out of the shadows and draw closer to the fishermen. Their coats reek of freshwater fish. Unchecked streams of perspiration trail from Simon's brow down his suntanned cheeks, then disappear within the folds of his thick beard. Andrew's sweat-stained shirt clings to his back. James and John, also appear haggard, their clothing damp and discolored with the residue of a night on the sea. They're tired, worn out from a night of toiling on the sea. Yet, they're laughing and talking loudly about their recent haul.

Another figure approaches. You squint your eyes against the sun, now higher in the sky. The face comes into focus. Jesus has come to the seashore.

He draws close to Simon and Andrew and beckons them. "Follow Me, and I will make you become fishers of men."

Without hesitation, they drop their nets and climb up the bank to where He is standing. They don't look back. They simply follow Him along the shoreline and approach James and John.

Like He did with Peter and Andrew, Jesus calls out, "Follow Me, and I will make you become fishers of men." Though the two brothers were probably looking forward to a long afternoon rest, as soon as Jesus summons them, they drop everything and rush to His side, leaving their father and the hired servants to finish the job.

You ponder the situation. Only the very wealthy are able to hire servants to assist in their labor, so James and John are not only walking away from their father, they are walking away from a lucrative business.

Jesus words have also pierced your heart. It's as if, while He has called the four of them, He's also called you. There on the shores of Galilee, Jesus is forming the beginning of His own small group of supporters.

Wherever He goes, He draws great crowds. He doesn't have to look for an audience. People flock to Him. They don't always need a synagogue or any other formal place to worship. The mountains and highways are sufficient. People can gather to hear Jesus' messages anywhere.

Now He has singled out a select few. Four men who will soon become part of a dozen who will walk with Him for the next three years. They'll also pray with Him and labor beside Him. Twelve men to carry on the gospel message long after Jesus returns to His home in heaven. Twelve men to serve as examples to those who will follow in future generations.

In much the same way, you have the a similar support system available to you, people who will pray with you and for you, people you can depend on for help in a time of need. And you can be there for them too. They're called small groups in some churches. Or home teams. Or community groups. They meet in each other's houses. They pray together. They dine together. They study the scriptures. They share a time of fellowship. They offer help when needed. They venture out together to serve in their communities and to seek and save the lost, just as Jesus and His disciples did.

Count yourself blessed if you have connected in such a way. For we are all fishers of men. Together we can cast a net into the sea of humanity and rescue the lost and lonely fish of the world.

"Be kindly affectionate to one another with brotherly love, in honor giving preference to one another; not lagging in diligence, fervent in spirit, serving the Lord; rejoicing in hope, patient in tribulation, continuing steadfastly in prayer, distributing to the needs of the saints, given to hospitality.

~Romans 12:10-13

Chapter Seven

AT THE WEDDING IN CANA WITH JESUS
Believe the Impossible

Reading: John 2:1-11

You're in Cana—"house of reeds"—a village in Galilee, situated in a grassy plain about four miles northeast of Nazareth. It would have taken Mary and Jesus almost two hours to travel by foot over rugged hills from their home in Nazareth. They've come to Cana for the wedding of a friend.

You've joined the other guests, including Jesus' disciples who were also invited. You share their anticipation as they await the arrival of the betrothed couple. They're coming from the bride's home. From this day on, she'll reside at the home of the groom.

A shout goes up in the crowd. Here they come, clothed in wedding attire—the bride in a pure white gown, a crown of flowers on her head and with a long, sheer veil, like a lacy waterfall covering her face and the front of her dress. The groom is wearing his finest tunic, and a white cloak embroidered with brilliant colors. He also has a floral crown on his head. They're both adorned with bracelets and jewels.

They're walking side-by-side, her hand resting on his forearm, a proud smile on his face. They were pledged to each other since childhood, and now they will consummate their marriage with a week-long feast, filled with music, red wine, and a table laid out with exotic foods.

You've already gotten caught up in the revelry. Flutes and lyres and tambourines pour out a rhythmic blend of instruments. Singers add to the mix with songs of love, many of them gleaned from the Song of Solomon. All around you, people chatter happily. They laugh, they sing, they dance. They offer presents and shower words of blessing on the young couple.

You walk about the courtyard in your own special robe, furnished by your host for the occasion. You sample sweet barley cakes and pungent olives, sizzling lamb and roasted vegetables, raisins, apples, and grapes, arranged on silver trays. Like the other guests, you recline on a mat, taste sweet pastries, and sip the glass of wine that never seems to go dry. Then, responding to a friend's call, you leap from the ground and join the celebrants in a lively circle dance around the bride and groom.

But, suddenly, word has arisen that all of the wine has been consumed and the barrels are empty. The stewards search frantically for more. Your host hurries about, his face red with distress, his fingers plucking at his beard in frustration.

Mary of Nazareth is watching as the celebration turns into a terrible fiasco. It would be disgraceful for the bridegroom if he does not produce more wine for his guests. Still calm in the midst of all the panic, Mary quietly draws close to Jesus.

"They have no wine," she whispers.

He hesitates. "Woman, what does your concern have to do with Me? My hour has not yet come."

Such a perplexing statement. First of all, Jesus has called His mother "woman." It sounds like an insult, but it couldn't be, not from Jesus. Mary's calm response indicates she was not offended, for she says to the stewards, "Whatever He says to you, do it."

Jesus orders the stewards to fill the six stone pots with water. It's strange that a simple carpenter should command such authority, but the young men follow His instructions. Each pot, filled to the brim, can hold twenty or thirty gallons of water, enough for everyone to bathe in if they desired.

You snicker with amusement. Jesus is promising water when the guests are calling for wine. You shake your head and wonder how long it will take for the master of the house to shut down the feast.

Still obviously in charge, Jesus tells the stewards to serve the head steward first. Cautiously, the head steward takes a sip from the cup, then he jerks back in amazement, and he quickly summons the bridegroom.

"Every man at the beginning sets out the good wine, and when the guests have well drunk, then the inferior," he says. "You have kept the good wine until now!"

Encouraged, you hold out your cup and sample the purple liquid yourself. Why, it's the best you've ever tasted. It doesn't reek of vinegar like wines that have been aged too long. It's not overly sweet, but has a mild, palatable flavor. Other guests flock to the waterpots and fill their cups. They smack their lips and sing out their approval.

You stare in awe at Jesus. He has done the impossible. "A miracle," someone says.

The thing is, just as He changed water into wine, He can change sinners into servants, ashes to beauty, mourning to laughter, despair into praise, and a broken vessel into a precious urn. Was the bridegroom's astonishment any greater than the astonishment one feels when they see a changed heart or a changed life? Like the stewards did, we only need to take the useless thing to the Lord and then watch what He can do with it.

For with God nothing will be impossible.

~Luke 1:37

Chapter Eight

AT NIGHT WITH NICODEMUS AND JESUS
One Way to God

Reading: John 3:1-17

Y ou've reached Jerusalem, the Holy City of God, where rituals abound and pilgrims come from all over Israel and beyond to celebrate three major feasts in the Jewish religion. It's the Passover now. Many visitors have traveled a great distance to celebrate the feast. Also faithful to His upbringing, Jesus has journeyed nearly ninty miles from His home in Capernaum.

Jerusalem and the surrounding villages have exploded with visitors. Once again, the inns are full to overflowing. The marketplace is crowded during the day as merchants haggle with buyers, doctors of the Law debate the scriptures, and shepherds pass through with bleating animals prepared for sacrifice. All day long, smoke rises from the temple's altar beyond the restrictive gate.

The hillsides outside the city also have come alive with visitors. Tents and campfires cover the ridge. With the setting of the sun the stifling heat of day has given place to bitter cold. The extreme change in weather is no surprise, for in one day you have experienced blazing sunshine and the taste of dust in the air, followed by a drizzle of rain, and now a frigid mist. Such is the unpredictable climate of the Middle East.

You draw your outer cloak tighter around your shoulders and trudge over the cobbled streets in search of Jesus. The courtyards of the wealthy tower on each side of the road. Vines cover the outside walls, their flowering petals closed up for the night. You make your way uphill and, at last, you find Him outside the temple wall in the shadow of a hackberry tree, with its knobby, aged trunk and its proliferation of green leaves and dark red berries.

Jesus is speaking with a Pharisee named Nicodemus. It's amazing

22

that a member of the Sanhedrin should make time to visit with this humble Galilean carpenter. Most of the religious leaders have shunned Jesus. They either avoid Him entirely or they engage Him in animated confrontations. Nicodemus has much to lose if his associates learn of this clandestine meeting. Some have even plotted to kill this man from Galilee.

And so, while many people approach Jesus in the light of day, this man has sought Him out under the cover of darkness. Nicodemus does not appear to be confrontational. Instead, he seems to have set aside the legalistic confines of his order, and he appears to be open to whatever Jesus has to say. How astounding that someone who's been entrenched in the teachings of Judaism and the more recent debilitating oral traditions appears to be captivated by Jesus' words.

With mounting interest, you step close enough to hear what they are saying. Nicodemus has addressed Jesus as "Rabbi," an honorific bestowed only on men of great learning. In a spirit of humility, this Pharisee has elevated Jesus to teacher, and he has reduced himself to student.

Even so, Jesus' message initially perplexes this learned man. The Lord speaks of being born of water and being born of the Spirit. Nicodemus frowns in puzzlement. Does Jesus mean the natural flow of water during a child's birth? Or is He simply referring to water baptism, like John the Baptist espoused? And why does He compare the Spirit of God with the movement of the wind? So many questions.

Jesus then challenges Nicodemus to move beyond what he already knows regarding earthly things and consider heavenly concepts. Then He comes to the main point. "For God so loved the world that He gave His only begotten Son, that whoever believes in Him should not perish but have everlasting life."

Jesus goes on to explain the difference between condemnation and salvation, light and darkness, evil deeds and the truth. The Pharisee listens quietly. He asks no more questions. Gives no argument. Refrains from doubt. As Nicodemus departs, pensive lines spread across his forehead. A subtle change has been wrought in this Pharisee.

For this meeting, Nicodemus came secretly, but one day he will step boldly before the Council and speak words of defense on behalf of Jesus. Afterward, he also will stand at the foot of the cross with embalming ointments in his hands, while another Pharisee, Joseph of Arimathaea, claims the body of Jesus for burial.

Nicodemus had witnessed the miracles. He had spoken with the Savior. Though Jesus' message initially confused him, in time he will fully comprehend what being born again means. He will move from darkness to light, from a mind filled with the teachings of man to a heart filled with the love of God.

Like Nicodemus, you've grown up with a particular religious background, or maybe none at all. Perhaps it's time you also moved from the shadows into the light. If you haven't already understood the concept of being born again, perhaps it's time. Search the scriptures. Read John Chapter 3, and consider God's word with an open heart.

For with the heart one believes unto righteousness, and with the mouth confession is made unto salvation.

~Romans 10:10

AT THE WELL IN SAMARIA WITH JESUS
Quenching Spiritual Thirst

Reading: John 4:1-14

As you travel with Jesus and His disciples from Jerusalem to Galilee, you will walk more than eighty miles through barren wilderness, with an occasional stop at an oasis. For this journey you wisely packed an extra pair of sandals, certain you'll wear out the first pair long before you reach your destination.

Immediately upon leaving the Holy City, you encounter the first stretch of a parched wasteland. It hasn't rained in a while. The hard-packed soil is riddled with cracks and crevices. Your sandals scrape along the surface, kicking dust into the air and filling your throat with the taste of sun-baked clay. The hot sun beats down on your head. Though you've wrapped your brow in a turban, you can't escape the steady sting of heat. You shade your eyes against the glare and wonder if the pool of water on the horizon is real or simply one of those desert apparitions you've heard about.

Soon your party reaches Samaria's hill country. It's a stark, mountainous area of Palestine. The gentle, rolling hills are quite different from the sheer cliffs of Judea. Only a few blades of grass poke out of the scorched ground. Farther ahead you see patches of green, a sign there may be a well nearby.

Centuries ago, this fertile place served as the headquarters for the kings of Israel. Though Samaria has long been a district of Palestine, people of strict Jewish faith generally avoid traveling through this part of the country, unwilling to mingle with the mixed race of people who reside here—half Jewish and half Gentile.

You've reached the midway point on the road to Galilee. Over the last three days, you've traveled forty-two miles on foot. You're tired and hungry. And thirsty.

Squinting against the sun's afternoon brilliance, you search for a place to rest. Breathing a sigh, you settle on a carpet of grass beneath the sheltering leaves of a palm tree, its fronds spreading overhead in a feathery canopy. A spattering of sunlight filters through the leaves and casts a scintillating pattern on the desert floor.

You scan the horizon. Nearby is Mount Gerizim. The Samaritans consider it the holiest place in the world, for it was here that Moses and the Israelites offered sacrifices after entering the Promised Land. Gerizim's summit is covered by a patchwork of shrubs. At the peak stand the ruins of an ancient temple. A rambling staircase ascends the mountain toward this ancient place of worship. At the base is Jacob's well, which the nation's patriarch deeded to his son Joseph.

An excited cry goes up from the group and several lunge ahead. Water! It's time to quench your thirst. You rise to your feet and follow Jesus and His company as they approach the rock-encased well. Huge blocks of rough-hewn stones form resting places for the weary travelers. A circle of flat rocks create a ledge around the well. Your lips parched and your water flask empty, you join the others for a taste of the sweet, clear liquid.

It is the sixth hour—12 o'clock noon. A woman has come there during this ungodly hour, the worst part of the day for drawing water or any other kind of hard labor. For that very reason, the women usually come early to the well, before the sun has begun to rise. But women who live unsavory lives come later in the day, when they can draw their water alone and avoid being shunned by the others. One lone woman has arrived, a veil covering her face. She lowers her pot into the water and draws it up, the precious liquid splashing over the side.

Jesus has remained at the well, but his disciples have gone to a nearby city to buy food. To your surprise, the Lord approaches the lone woman and asks her for a drink of water. It's unheard of for a Jew to strike up a conversation with a Samaritan, especially a woman.

But Jesus does not conform to man's rules of propriety. He has established His own standards for life, and He speaks to whomever He will.

"Whoever drinks of this water will thirst again," Jesus tells the woman. "But whoever drinks of the water that I shall give him will never thirst. But the water that I shall give him will become in him a fountain of water springing up into everlasting life."

Like the woman, you came to this well thirsty. But this kind of thirst cannot be quenched by the world's water. If your spiritual life seems parched and dying, perhaps you, too, need the "living water" Jesus offered the woman. It can be found within the scriptures. Every time you pick up the Bible and read, you're taking a life-saving drink. Ironically, the more you drink from the Word of God, the thirstier you will get.

If any man thirst, let him come to Me, and drink. He who believes in Me, as the Scripture has said, out of his heart will flow rivers of living water.

~John 7:37-38

Chapter Ten

IN THE SYNAGOGUE WITH JESUS
One's Hometown

Reading: Luke 4:16-30

Yyou've returned to Nazareth, the place where Jesus spent His youth. In recent years, He moved to Capernaum, but He often returns to His hometown. You have a good idea where you might find Him. In the synagogue.

Of course, the temple in Jerusalem is ten times larger and far grander than any of the synagogues throughout the land. And this synagogue is much smaller than most of the others. But today it holds a special significance, for it is Saturday morning, the Sabbath, and the Lord of all the Earth has come there to read from the scriptures.

Like other synagogues in Israel, the one in Nazareth was built on the highest part of this foothill community. The square, boxlike facade is constructed of rocks and mortar with limestone lintels framing the only door. The front of the building faces toward the south, where, though unable to be seen at this distance, stands the city of Jerusalem. Similarly, all the synagogues in the land are constructed to face the Temple.

You approach with a sense of awe. Quietly, you step inside and pause at the top of a set of stone steps. You've moved from the sun-laden heat of day into a refreshing coolness. There is no dampness in this cave-like interior. Candles cast a muted glow on the altar, a broad, waist-high table and behind it, a niche in the wall where the precious scrolls are kept. The aroma of warmed olive oil permeates the air. You savor its calming essence, and pray quietly.

Makeshift benches fill the room. People have already arrived from all parts of Galilee. They slide onto the benches, their voices stilled. The air seems charged with energy, like something special is going to happen.

It's the Sabbath day. The service begins with a recitation of the Shema and prayers led by the synagogue ruler. Then, he steps aside and offers a scroll of Isaiah to the learned men in the audience. Jesus accepts the invitation, rises from the front bench, and mounts the two stairs to the altar. He moves behind the table and receives the scroll, a roll of parchment made from several animal skins sewn together and wrapped around two separate rods.

Jesus carefully spreads the scroll and begins to read. Other than Jesus' voice, the only sounds are the steady breathing of the men sitting on the benches and the occasional murmurs of the women and young children, separated behind a lattice divider in the back of the room.

The passage in Isaiah speaks about the Spirit of the Lord resting upon the anointed, miracles of healing, and restoration of the oppressed. When Jesus finishes the reading, He takes the seat of Moses, a cumbersome chair carved out of a block of stone. It serves as a place of authority for whoever sits there. Jesus' next words stun the audience. He tells them the scriptures have been fulfilled in their hearing. By doing so, He has claimed to be the long-awaited Messiah.

"Is this not Joseph's son?" one says, remembering the young boy who'd grown up in the village, the child who once sat at the feet of a rabbi in this very synagogue, the same youth who worked in His father's carpentry shop.

Jesus does not falter. "Assuredly, I say to you, no prophet is accepted in his own country." Then He reminds the crowd of miracles that took place in the land of Israel. How a widow woman was saved from starvation, and a leper was healed of his disease. But not everyone can receive such miracles, Jesus admits. You watch in horror as angry men chase Him out of the synagogue. The sad thing is, they think they're being righteous.

With great concern, you rush after them, nearly tripping on the uneven stairs as you leave the synagogue. You follow them to the edge of the hill and catch your breath as they threaten to cast Jesus off the cliff.

Miraculously, He has slipped from their grasp and is walking away. You watch Him leave with deep sadness. Instead of throwing Jesus off the cliff, these people have thrown away their one chance to know the truth. They had sat in that same synagogue, week after week, had heard the reading of the prophecies, but still they don't understand.

Perhaps you have experienced a similar frustration when trying to reach your loved ones with the gospel of Jesus Christ. They also knew you as a child. They're aware of your shortcomings. They recall your failures and whims of fancy. You've tried to give them a precious pearl which they've rejected.

Though Jesus walked away, He didn't go far. He remained in Galilee, preaching and teaching the crowds that followed Him. He kept doing miracles. He didn't give up, and nor should you. There's no telling how much of what you say has been stored away. You may reach your loved ones when you least expect it.

And let us not grow weary while doing good, for in due season we shall reap if we do not lose heart.

~Galatians 6:9

Chapter Eleven

IN CAPERNAUM WITH JESUS
Walking in the Light

Reading: Matthew 4:12-17

Y ou've learned that Jesus, now 30 years old and rejected by the people of Nazareth, has moved to Capernaum, about eighteen miles away.

Capernaum is a highly prosperous town on the north shore of Galilee within the territory of Zebulun and Naphtali, also known as *Galilee of the Gentiles.* Though Jacob awarded this area to two of his sons, it's populated by multiple religions that are involved in idol worship. The prophet Isaiah spoke about a great light coming to this land, badly needed, for it has been steeped in spiritual darkness for centuries.

More than 1,500 people reside in Capernaum, many of them are fishermen, farmers, and craftsmen. The city sits on a major trade route between Damascus and Egypt. Numerous caravans stop here bringing tourists and merchants who barter with the local businesses and bring much prosperity to the region.

You've traveled here in search of Jesus. "Why would He come here?" you ask a passer-by. "Why did He not remain in Nazareth?"

The stranger raises his eyebrows, surprised that you should ask. "Herod rules the area surrounding Nazareth," he explains. "He would kill Jesus if given the chance." He offers a wide, sweeping gesture that takes in the city on the hill and the sea. "But here," he says, "anyone can wander about and preach whatever he chooses. Philip rules this land, and he tolerates the different religions. Your Jesus is safe here."

You stroll along the sandy, rock-strewn coast and breathe deeply of the salty air wafting off the sea. A Roman garrison has taken over a section of the land. Armed mercenaries stand guard over the tax center and closely watch the publicans. Plumed soldiers march about, their boots crunching on the path, their shields glistening in the brightness of day. Like everyone else, you step aside and let them pass.

Blazing sunlight reflects off the white stone of the pillared synagogue on the hill. You shade your eyes against the glare. Then you see Him, leading a crowd of followers from place to place, touring the area as though on an important mission. He speaks words of comfort to a centurion who expressed concern for an ill servant.

Jesus' fame has traveled everywhere. Great multitudes have come from throughout the land, from Galilee and Decapolis, and even as far away as Jerusalem and beyond the Jordan. People bring friends and relatives who are sick with different diseases or plagued by devils. To your amazement, He heals them all.

You join the crowd and listen closely as Jesus tells parable after parable, heals one person after another, and ministers to the spiritually lost and the physically hurting, even raising from a death bed the daughter of Jairus, the synagogue leader.

Eventually, Capernaum will be called The Lord's City, most likely because Jesus performed more miracles here than anywhere else during His three-year ministry on earth. Like Isaiah predicted, He was drawn to this place because of the intense darkness. Doesn't that make sense? Doesn't the light shine brightest where the darkness is most pronounced? Hasn't Jesus been called the Light of the world?

Only days before John the Baptist was arrested. Jesus came here after saying the time had been fulfilled and the kingdom of God was at hand. Now He's the one calling for repentance. And He's promising the only kind of light that can break through spiritual darkness. The only light that can illuminate the minds of those who have fallen prey to false religions and, for some, no religion at all.

Zebulon and Naphtali are not unique. People live in many dark places. Spiritual darkness can sweep into any city, any country, any home. It can invade a school, a place of business, even a church. It always has and always will. But we've been blessed with a light that can dispel that kind of darkness.

Perhaps you work in a spiritually dark place. Or perhaps a

spiritual darkness has taken over your neighborhood or your city. Unconfessed or unaddressed sin can keep people trapped in that darkness. So can unnatural ties to the world.

Though we may solve all of our worldly problems, we cannot rescue people from spiritual darkness—not without Jesus. The first chapter of the Gospel of John says Jesus is the true Light that lights every man who comes into the world. Repentance is the beginning. It can shed the glow of understanding on a dark place. Trusting in Christ is like flipping a wall switch that will never turn off.

Seek the true light for yourself, and then offer it to others through acts of kindness and words of comfort. Don't hide your light under a bushel, but set it on a high hill to illuminate the world around you.

"I am the light of the world. He who follows Me shall not walk in darkness, but have the light of life."

~John 8:12

Chapter Twelve

IN THE BOAT WITH JESUS I
A New Calling

Reading: Luke 5:1-11

Once again, you have ventured onto the banks of Galilee, in the northern part Israel. Awestruck, you peer out over the pear-shaped stretch of water. It's huge, twelve and a half miles long and seven and a half miles wide. Also called Chinnereth, or the Lake of Tiberius, this body of water is known for sudden uprisings.

For the moment, the water rests, flat and serene, like a plate of glass. At the lake's edge, weary fishermen stagger out of the sea, exhausted after a fruitless night of trawling. They moor their boats. They spread their nearly empty nets and dump a mere handful of flailing fish on the shore. The shimmering scales set off a rainbow of sparkles into the glow of the rising sun.

Several fishermen gather. They are Simon Peter and his brother Andrew, Thomas, who one day will be known as The Doubter, Nathaniel—also called Bartholomew, Philip, and two brothers, James and John, the sons of Zebedee.

Their leathery faces speak of long hours battling the elements. Their linen shirts reek of fish entrails. Their hands bear the bloody cuts of the sharp-edged knives they use to clean their catch—when there is one.

Today, they have little to show for a long night spent on the sea. The fishermen hunch over their seines and wash them free of weeds and debris. They'll patch the holes, mend the netting, and hang them to dry on a line. Their boats stand idle now, emitting a subtle groaning of wood against wood.

Suddenly, a shadow falls across your path, and a chill travels down your spine. You know without looking. It's Jesus. Voices cause you to turn. Behind Him is a crowd of people—an odd mix of nobility and commoners. You eye them with interest. You could easily be lost amidst this multitude.

When you turn back toward the sea, you find that Jesus has moved down the hill and is already climbing into Simon's boat. He's ordering the big fisherman to take his vessel away from shore. Andrew already has climbed aboard along with their hired men. James and John do the same and fill their own boat with a crew.

Quickly, before Simon can set sail, you stumble down the slope and splash into the water. A gentle froth oozes into your sandals and soaks the hem of your garment. You strain against the water's pull and climb onto Simon's boat, a twenty-seven-foot-long construction of cedar and oak, light enough to be swept along with a gust of wind, but strong enough to withstand the violence of the sea.

As Simon pushes off, you settle onto a plank of wood. The boat drifts away from the shore, rocking from side-to-side. You relax with the gentle sway, confident with the knowledge the Savior is on board.

The craft drifts a little way onto the lake. At Jesus' command, Simon drops the anchor. The boat is close enough to the shore for the crowd to hear Him speak. When He ends His discourse, He tells Simon to launch farther out. Again, the big fisherman obeys, this time drifting to the center of the lake where the depth is close to 150 feet. The other boats follow. Satisfied, Jesus tells Simon to let down his net.

The burly fisherman protests. "Master, we have toiled all night and caught nothing." Then he gives a shrug. "Nevertheless, at Your word I will let down the net."

Following Simon's lead, the other fishermen also unravel their nets, adjust the heavy weights around the edges, and cast their woven blankets into the sea. The nets disappear beneath the surface and sink to the bottom. Then the quiet morning erupts with cries of surprise. The fishermen leap into action, pulling on the thick cords to raise the nets, now straining with a heavy weight. The webbing starts to come apart. The men struggle to preserve the nets and save their catch. You rise up to help. The cord slips through your fingers. The weight is too strong, too difficult to hold on.

Grunting and straining, Peter and his crew hoist the net up and over the side of the boat. Mounds of fish tumble at your feet. Excited voices rise above the splash of the waves. The spray tickles your lips and soaks into your clothing. You're standing in ankle-high water filled with hundreds of flailing fish, each of them a good six inches long.

Overwhelmed with gratitude, Simon falls to his knees before Jesus.

"Do not be afraid," the Savior tells him. "From now on you will catch men."

Jesus' statement gets you thinking. Catch men instead of fish? You consider your own friends and family members. Perhaps you've attempted to reach them before, but some have rejected your message. Just like He did with Simon, Jesus may be telling you not to give up. Perhaps, like Simon, you also need to launch out into the deep and cast your net a second time, and a third. Who knows? You may also witness a miracle.

Go into all the world and preach the gospel to every creature.
~Mark 16:15

Chapter Thirteen

IN PETER'S HOUSE WITH JESUS
Caring for Loved Ones

Reading: Matthew 8:14-15

Y ou've been invited to the home of Simon Peter. Originally from Bethsaida, he has settled in Capernaum with his wife and his mother-in-law.

You approach their house, a two-story, mud-brick structure that is larger than most of the other homes in the village. A wooden stairway runs straight up the outer wall to a flat roof with a two-foot protective railing all the way around.

Every morning and every evening, Peter can stand on his roof and look at the sky for the signs. Red sky at night means clear weather is due. But a red sky at dawn means a storm is imminent. Even so, the signs don't always tell the truth. Not in Galilee, where the fairest of weather conditions can change in an instant.

Peter's house has two courtyards. One contains a modest garden of vegetables and herbs. There's a round oven for roasting meat and a fire pit for searing fish. The other courtyard serves as a shelter for Peter's goat and donkey and a place for storing his fishing gear. The smell of freshly scaled fish permeates the air, and the worn pavement bears the bloody stains of his latest catch.

You follow Jesus and His disciples into the house, stooping slightly to clear the five-foot-high doorway. Narrow windows set high on the wall allow for enough light to brighten the main room during the daytime. Several candle stands are positioned about the room to be lit at night. Thick tapestries ensure privacy to a number of sleeping quarters for family and guests.

The furnishings reveal a humble, yet formidable lifestyle. Woven mats and pillows for reclining. A raised table that stands a foot off the floor for dining. A wooden bench where guests can sit to have their feet washed by their host. And numerous niches in the kitchen wall for storing food and cooking utensils.

A fire blazes on the indoor hearth where two large pots remain empty and waiting. Nearby stands a water pot. Shelves line one wall bearing baskets, bowls, and jars, plus sacks of grain, dried fruit, and spices. But there is no cooking today, for Peter's mother-in-law has fallen ill with a severe fever, and his wife is pressing a damp cloth to her mother's forehead.

The ailing woman is reclining on a straw-filled mattress with a light blanket pulled up to her chin. Upon entering, Jesus moves toward her and reaches for her hand. He whispers a few words, and seconds later, her fever is gone and she rises, refreshed and ready to serve her guests. As always when Jesus performs a miracle, a sense of awe settles over the gathering. The disciples murmur among themselves. Peter's wife, falls gratefully at Jesus' feet.

Miraculously transformed, Peter's mother-in-law bustles about the kitchen as if no illness had overtaken her. She dips liquid from the large waterpot and fills a kettle that once stood empty. She tosses pieces of fish in the kettle, then adds chopped vegetables— leeks and potatoes, and pungent herbs. A delectable aroma rises with the steam.

A few minutes later, she ladles the contents into a large serving bowl, which she places on the table. Meanwhile, Peter's wife has been gathering unleavened bread from a warming place on the hearth. She places them in two baskets and brings them to the table. Then she hurries to add a bottle of wine and a platter of fruit and cheese.

At Peter's beckoning, you and the others sit on woven mats around the table. Peter's mother-in-law surveys the setting, then, satisfied, she steps back, her hands clasped in front of her, a healthy smile on her lips.

After Peter blesses the meal, his guests fill their earthenware bowls with stew from the pot. You do the same and then reach for a piece of bread to dip into the broth. You raise it, dripping, to your mouth and savor the salty taste of fish and vegetables.

You ponder the miracle of healing that took place only minutes before. And you notice something else. Peter has demonstrated the importance of caring for family and especially for the elderly.

In a sense, Peter was saying, "I love you" when he invited his mother-in-law to live in his home. He was saying, "I love you," when he cared for her while she was sick. And he was saying, "I love you," when he brought Jesus to her bedside.

At some time in life, we all have the opportunity to care for someone who is ill or aging. We may watch our parents and their siblings grow old and helpless. One day, they will become the child, and we will become the adult. Just as they cared for us in our infancy, we have the opportunity to care for them in their infirmity. Most importantly, like Peter did, we can bring Jesus to them. In all these things, we are saying, "I love you."

But if anyone does not provide for his own, and especially for those of his household, he has denied the faith, and is worse than an unbeliever.

~1 Timothy 5:8

Chapter Fourteen

AT MATTHEW'S HOME WITH JESUS
Socializing with the Lost

Reading: Matthew 9:9-13

Once again you're in Capernaum, this time in the heart of town near the toll center where tax collectors—mostly Jewish men—are bringing in the day's revenues for the Romans. A man named Levi sits at one of the booths. The men in line mumble curses beneath their breath. Like many tax collectors—or publicans—Levi has often been accused of charging more than the required tax and lining his own pockets with the extra funds.

Over the months, he has developed a thick skin and doesn't seem to care what his neighbors think of him. When his workday ends, he mingles with other tax collectors, drinking and dining to his heart's content, for his work has made him one of the wealthiest men in the city.

By setting up his booth along the road that runs between Damascus and Accho, Levi collects revenues from the fishermen who toil on the Sea of Galilee, as well as farmers who plant and harvest in the nearby fields and merchants who sell their wares in the city. No one escapes the wary eye of the tax collector.

You draw close to Levi's stand and peer over his shoulder. Although he's employed by the Romans, he has refrained from using the cumbersome Roman numerals and has chosen instead to record his transactions using the Greek system of numbering, which is far more legible to people of any nationality.

You turn your ear to the line of merchants who've come to pay their taxes. The fee for regular items, such as household goods, produce, and fish is five percent of the sale. Luxury items bring in a much larger tax at twelve and a half percent. These people are not happy. You catch snippets of whispered insults. Several refer to Levi with such derogatory terms as "traitor" and "thief" and "worst of sinners."

A fishermen leans close to you. The smell of a fresh catch floats off his clothing. "We have to watch these filthy publicans," he snarls, his eyes fastened on Levi. "They often charge a higher toll than is required by law."

The man opens his fist, exposing several denarii bearing the image of Caesar. "I have the exact amount," he says with a wink, then he quickly closes his fist over the coins. "If we don't bring the correct amount, we lose the difference, for we must never accept change from these filthy dogs. Their money is unclean. If we don't have the right amount, we borrow the difference from a friend."

At that moment, Jesus cuts into the line and provokes a rise of complaints from the waiting merchants. He ignores the grumbling and boldly steps up to Levi's table. Then He does something astounding. He invites Levi to leave his booth and follow Him. The protests grow louder as Levi rises from the seat of customs and accompanies Jesus. He's left behind the record book and several stacks of coins. Immediately, a Roman overseer rushes down and passes Levi's work to another tax collector.

There's no need to linger at the house of customs. Levi has walked away with Jesus and His disciples. Increasing your step, you follow them past the Plain of Gennesaret, a fertile swath of land where stalks of wheat and barley wave, stirred by a gentle breeze. Staying close behind the others, you climb the limestone ridge and follow a winding street past houses clustered together in a pristine grouping of wealth. There's the house where Jesus healed Peter's mother. Ahead stands an elaborate home with a large courtyard. Pink flowering bougainvillea frame the entrance. White sprays of jasmine blanket the outer wall, emitting their intoxicating perfume into the street. This is the dwelling of a very rich man.

Levi ushers his guests inside. A group of his associates—publicans and known sinners—follow, with Jesus and His disciples in their midst. Within a short time, several of Levi's servants are spreading a grand feast before the large crowd.

Meanwhile, several Pharisees have gathered outside and are

peppering Jesus' disciples with questions. They accuse Jesus of breaking the Law by socializing with publicans and sinners. The disciples convey the message to Jesus. His response both amazes and convicts you.

"They who are whole do not need a physician, but they that are sick."

Jesus isn't speaking about physical illness. He's concerned for a man's spiritual wellbeing. By this time, Jesus has begun calling his host *Matthew,* which translates to *Gift of God.* He's looking past the thankless job, the elaborate home, the fine clothing.

Similarly, you may want to think about the people you come across every day—the rich and the poor, the sick and the well, the imprisoned and the free. Perhaps it's time to put aside any bias or fears you might have and reach out to someone. In God's kingdom, there is no caste system, no prejudice. Only souls in need of a Savior.

And the King will answer and say to them, 'Assuredly, I say to you, inasmuch as you did it to one of the least of these My brethren, you did it to Me.'

~Matthew 25:40

Chapter Fifteen

IN THE BOAT WITH JESUS II
The Storms of Life

Reading: Mark 4:35-41

It's late in the day, the usual time when the fishermen launch out on the Sea of Galilee. You walk along the coastline amidst the rocks and stretches of sand. You breathe in the salty air and scan the shoreline, looking for the disciples. Simon is releasing the ropes. If you don't want to be left behind, you must hurry and climb aboard. You step forward. Ripples of water lap into your sandals and soak the hem of your garment.

As you step into Peter's boat, the old wooden vessel groans and lists to one side. You settle on a plank of wood, then you relax beneath the caress of a gentle breeze. As the boat drifts lazily out onto the water, all seems peaceful and serene.

Yet, you've heard the Sea of Galilee is an awesome mystery. Its blue-green water lies deceptively tranquil for now. One minute the sea looks like glass and appears to be sleeping. The next minute it awakens with a vengeance that can overturn boats and drown everyone aboard. Such are the tales that have come back from the sea.

Jesus' disciples are no strangers to the phenomenon. Those who live in the coastal cities of Bethsaida and Capernaum grew up amidst the stories surrounding the Sea of Galilee, also known as Tiberius. Though they've become accustomed to the sudden stirring of the lake, they cannot predict Galilee's unexpected changes of weather.

A warning now. Don't get too comfortable. The sea of glass has begun to stir. The wind has gained strength. Now your boat begins to rock from side to side. You grip the board underneath you just before a surge of waves threatens to overturn the vessel. A flash of lightning raises the hair on your arms, and a clash of thunder nearly sends you cowering to the floor.

A blanket of dark clouds is gathering overhead, blotting out the sprinkle of stars that moments ago dominated the sky. A sudden burst of wind takes your breath away. The water's surface is erupting in tiny spikes. A spray of seawater pricks your face. The boat lurches. You grab onto the side and hold on.

You look to the disciples for some consolation. They've already sprung into action. Andrew is standing at the bow, his forehead lined with concern, his eyes trained on the darkness ahead. Peter leaps to his feet and draws close to his brother. Together they search for an opening in the surging tide. Philip drops the net he's been repairing and reaches for an oar. Others hang on, terror filling their eyes, their mouths open, their cries smothered by the screaming storm.

Swirling black clouds open their gnarled fingers and release bullets of rain on the sea. A sudden wave tosses your boat like a toy. There's a bright flash and a deafening thud, followed by another surge of water drenching everyone in the boat. Then, just when it seems it couldn't get any worse, the raging sea turns even more violent. Wind shrieks in your ears and drives daggers of salty seawater against your face. Your outer garment, soaked and limp, clings to your back. Strands of your hair stick to your face. Your heart pounding, you stare through the veil of teeming rain. The opposite shore remains a great distance away, barely visible between the sheets of dark rainwater.

In a panic, one of the disciples asks where Jesus has gone. Another points to the back of the boat. While the disciples are trying to get their craft under control, the Master sleeps. Two of them stumble toward the back of the rocking boat. Their voices sail to you on the wind. "Teacher, do You not care that we are perishing?"

A cry lodges in your throat. If Jesus can ignore the disciples' pleas, what hope do you have? You've experienced other storms of life. Why would Jesus help you with the problem at work? Why would He concern Himself with your bank account, or bother to heal your ailing child? Then you realize, while you've been trying to fix your own problems, He's been there all along. But He isn't sleeping. You only need to call on Him.

At that moment, Jesus calmly rises from His pillow and stands to His feet. In a voice filled with authority He utters only three words.

"Peace, be still!"

Immediately, the wind dies down. The sea settles to its former glassiness. The clouds pull away and expose a starlit sky. A full moon reveals the opposite shore's long arms spread in a friendly welcome.

Jesus shakes his head at His disciples. "Why are you so fearful? How is it that you have no faith?"

His words pierce your own heart, and you wonder what will happen the next time a storm disrupts your life. How will you deal with situations that appear to be out of your control? Will you behave like Jesus' disciples and stumble about, wailing like a helpless child? Will you try to fix the problem yourself, or will you trust the One who is able to command the wind and the sea—He who has promised never to leave or forsake you will surely carry you to the other side?

For God has not given us a spirit of fear, but of power and of love and of a sound mind.

~2 Timothy 1:7

Chapter Sixteen

AT THE POOL OF BETHESDA WITH JESUS
Breaking the Rules

Reading: John 5:1-16

Come to the Pool of Bethesda and witness another miracle. To get there, you must pass through the Sheep Gate, an opening at the far northeastern corner of the city. It's called the Sheep Gate because this is where shepherds bring their sheep to be sacrificed. They wash them in the pool and then present the unblemished animals to the priests.

After passing through the Sheep Gate, you enter the reservoir, a rectangular, rock-hewn construction with five huge porticos and pools at different levels, connected by a series of rock ledges and passageways. The chasm is fed by fresh rainwater and also by tiny streams that seep through cracks in the rock wall. A hot mist rises from the red-tinted pools, giving off the unmistakable odor of sulfur and other minerals.

All around, sitting on the ledges and lying on the hard, cold pavement, diseased bodies await the stirring of the water. Observers are leaning against the wall or the massive archways. The sick wait, eager to be the first in the pool when an angel comes to trouble the water, as the legend says.

With the arrival of Jesus, you forget about the body odors and the noxious smell of the water. He walks directly to a miserable invalid who's lying on a thin mat, woven from coarse plant fibers and camel's hair. The ground beneath him is a short distance from the pool, but he's been plagued by this unknown illness for 38 years, and he cannot move. Nor does anyone help him into the water when it stirs.

Instead of offering to carry the man into the pool, Jesus simply asks him a question. "Do you want to be made well?"

Now, who would say no to that question? Of course, the man wants to be made whole. But, whenever the waters move, someone else steps down ahead of him.

Jesus responds with a command. "Rise, take up your bed and walk."

"Impossible," you say.

Nevertheless, the man immediately stands to his feet and picks up his mat. He's been healed without having stepped one foot in the water.

You marvel at the simplicity of it all. One word from Jesus. One command. And the man has been healed.

Fascinated, you follow the man into the temple. Moments later, the Jewish authorities catch him there carrying his mat. Horrors! It is the Sabbath. The Pharisees pressure him to tell them who healed him. It's as if they already know the answer and merely want confirmation. One more affront to add to the list they've already been compiling against Jesus.

The man tells them Jesus healed him, that He said to pick up his bed and walk. The Pharisees turn their wrath away from the man and focus on the Son of God.

Jesus has knowingly placed Himself in danger. He has incited the Jewish leaders. They accuse Him of breaking the Sabbath, but Jesus, the Son of God, has always obeyed the Father's commandments and He teaches His followers to do the same. Ironically, it's the Pharisees, His very accusers, who have broken God's Laws, time and time again. They have added their own restrictions to the written commandments, breaking God's command not to add anything to the scriptures.

Jesus, however, follows the spirit of the Law and not man's unreasonable interpretations. This isn't the first time He took such liberties on the Sabbath. There was that time when He allowed His hungry disciples to eat grains of wheat when they passed through a farmer's field. And the time He approved pulling an animal out of a pit on the Sabbath to save the beast's life. And those many times He emphasized the importance of loving one's neighbor over man's senseless rules and restrictions.

Jesus honored the Sabbath as it was ordained by God. What

He couldn't tolerate was man's distortion of God's commandment to "honor the Sabbath day." He saw the Sabbath as a wonderful blessing, not a day of enslavement to the rules of men.

In your own walk of faith, what does the Sabbath mean to you? For the Jew, the Sabbath is a 24-hour period from sundown on Friday to sundown on Saturday. For the Christian, the Sabbath is often Sunday, the first day of the week and the day Jesus was resurrected from the grave.

In the beginning, God rested on the seventh day from all the work He had done in creation. He instituted the Sabbath commandment so we also could take a time of rest from our daily work. It really doesn't matter what day you select or what you choose to do on that day. It's a gift from God. For Jesus, it was an opportunity to do good. That's what it should be for us too. Instead of being bogged down by senseless restrictions, we can approach the Sabbath in an attitude of peace and rest, no matter what we're actually doing.

And He said to them, "The Sabbath was made for man, and not man for the Sabbath."

~Mark 2:27

Chapter Seventeen

ON A HIGH MOUNTAIN WITH JESUS
Blessings for Life

Reading: Matthew 5:1-12

Travel now to the northwestern shore of Galilee and the Karazin Plateau, a grassy mound that is actually an extinct volcano. Below stands the sparkling lake, and beyond, the rugged cliffs of the Golan Heights. A swath of rich agricultural land stretches to the south. Stalks of wheat and barley sway with the breeze. Smaller plants bear clumps of lentils, pea pods, and melons. Full grape vines wind up trellises, ready for picking.

All around are reminders of Jesus' ministry to the people of Galilee. Nazareth, the home of His mother and brothers and the place where Jesus spent His early years. Cana, where He did His first miracle by turning water into wine. Capernaum, where the fishermen lowered their nets into the sea and brought out a great haul of fish. Tiberius, where Jesus taught crowds from a boat moored a short distance off shore.

With Jesus' expected return to this place the atmosphere has come alive as His followers wait in anticipation. You also have come to the mountain. You recline on the grassy slope. A great many of Jesus' disciples have gathered there—not only the original twelve, but many more men and women who have followed after Him. Conversations abound, and you wonder if you'll be able to hear Jesus' voice over the din.

But there is no need for concern. The moment the Lord reaches the hill, an uncanny silence descends upon the gathering. It gets so quiet you can hear the chirp of a cricket in the brush and the peeping of baby birds high in a sycamore tree.

All eyes are on the Master as He climbs to the top and settles there on a large rock. Without hesitation, He opens His mouth to speak. You listen with rapt attention as He promises eight blessings along with advice on how to receive them.

Blessed are the poor in spirit, For theirs is the kingdom of heaven.

Considering Jesus' past teachings, it's obvious He is not talking about the loss of material wealth. Poor in spirit has to mean something else. Forget about your bank account, your possessions, your many accomplishments, anything that may keep you from being poor in spirit. For the moment, come empty to the Lord.

Blessed are those who mourn, For they shall be comforted.

You already know what it means to mourn. Perhaps, you lost a loved one. A job. Maybe a long-held dream. You can freely mourn knowing that Jesus promises comfort.

Blessed are the meek, For they shall inherit the earth.

It's been said that meekness is not the same as weakness, that meekness is actually strength under control. The Bible gives two examples of that kind of meekness. Moses, the meekest man on earth—Numbers 12:3, and Jesus, for He's demonstrated what it's like to have the power and yet choose not to use it.

Blessed are those who hunger and thirst for righteousness, For they shall be filled.

Like being poor of spirit and being meek, this is a different kind of hunger and thirst from what the world teaches. It's not about the ache in your stomach or the dryness of your throat. These hunger pangs go deeper. This kind of thirst touches the heart, the very core of a person, and only the righteousness of God can satisfy.

Blessed are the merciful, For they shall obtain mercy.

Such a promise is similar to being forgiven as we forgive others, or receiving kindness on the same level as we have shown it. There is a do-unto-others concept of mercy. Unless we give it, we shouldn't expect to receive it.

Blessed are the pure in heart, For they shall see God.

Pure of heart? Perhaps painful events have hardened your heart over the years. It seems that only a little child can be pure of heart. They have not yet experienced the trials that come with growing up. Is it any wonder then that Jesus said we must come to Him like little children—innocent and trusting and pure of heart?

Blessed are the peacemakers, For they shall be called the sons of God.
You don't need to go to war to seek opportunities to make peace. Closer to home are many stages of conflict in need of a peacemaker who can step up and make things right. The battle may be in your backyard, or your workplace, or your own living room. Be a peacemaker whenever and wherever you can.

Blessed are those who are persecuted for righteousness' sake, For theirs is the kingdom of heaven.

If you will be strong in the Lord, you can expect opposition. You can expect persecution. Don't falter. For rewards await you in heaven. Refreshed and your heart brimming with promises of blessings, you now can lean back and take in the rest of Jesus' sermon, for He has many more lessons to teach.

> *I will make them and the places all around My hill a blessing;*
> *and I will cause showers to come down in their season; there*
> *shall be showers of blessing.*
>
> *~Ezekiel 34:26*

Chapter Eighteen

ON THE COAST OF TYRE AND SIDON WITH JESUS
Settling for Crumbs

Reading: Matthew 15:21-28

Journey now to the coast of the Mediterranean Sea and the area of Tyre and Sidon. These two prominent merchant cities produced timber, oils, metals, and an elegant purple dye harvested from the salt water mollusks. A strong smell of seaweed and fish wafts off the water, and the air is fresh and cool.

A vast rocky cliff descends from the western slope of Tyre, looking very much like a jagged waterfall. No surprise, for the word Tyre means "rock," a reflection of the city's defensive border of rocks and stones less than a mile from the shoreline.

The area's historic significance is well-known. This is where David formed a trade allowance with the merchants who sailed across the sea. This was the home of Hiram, who provided materials and workmen to help build Solomon's temple.

As you depart from the sea and move father inland, the smell of the sea gives way to the aroma of orange blossoms from a nearby grove and the pungent scent of cedar trees growing tall and straight along the roadway.

You've come here looking for Jesus. You find him grieving over a report that His cousin, John the Baptist, has perished through an order by Herod Antipas. Himself plagued by growing attacks from the religious leaders of Jerusalem, Jesus has come here in search of seclusion. This may be the only time He has traveled outside the boundaries of Palestine.

Now He's come to a territory primarily occupied by Gentiles, and He's approached by a Canaanite woman who's heard of His ability to perform miracles. Having heard about His presence there, she's traveled from the coast, falls at His feet, and begs for mercy. She acknowledges Him as Lord and asks Him to release her daughter from a demonic attack.

Though Jewish culture demands that women remain in the home, serving as wife and mother, Jesus has always respected the females who followed Him through the streets of Jerusalem and beyond. But those women were Jews. This one is a Gentile, and, whether man or woman, they are commonly shunned by the Jews.

Appalled by her insolence, the disciples try to shoo her away. Jesus also remains steadfast in His commitment to reach the "lost sheep of the house of Israel."

But the woman persists. Her long, black hair clings to the tears on her cheeks. Her brow is knotted with concern for her child. She kneels in the dirt of the road, soiling her richly embroidered dress, and pleads with Jesus to help.

His answer seems cold. "It is not good to take the children's bread and throw it to the little dogs."

She could slink away, disappointed and humiliated. Instead, her response comes from a meek and humble heart. "Yes, Lord," she says. "Yet the little dogs eat the crumbs which fall from their masters' table."

Moved by her faith, Jesus assures her that her daughter has been made whole that very hour.

You've watched the exchange with bated breath. If Jesus would respond favorably to that woman's petition, wouldn't He also lend an ear to your pleadings? If He would comfort an unbeliever, wouldn't He rush to your aide when you need Him? Is anything too hard for the Lord? Is anyone beyond His reach?

Perhaps it's time you took a moment to lay your needs at the foot of Jesus' cross, the way Christian did in *Pilgrim's Progress*. The Canaanite woman came humbly to Jesus. Yet she boldly asked for His help. It's a strange mix, isn't it? Boldness tempered by humility.

Like the Canaanite woman, you can bring your concerns to Jesus, no matter how big or small. Nothing is beyond the Lord's reach. He still works miracles today. Though not all of your prayers will be answered the way you hope, they are nevertheless answered. Sometimes the answer is yes, sometimes it's no, sometimes it's wait. The point is that you present your needs to Jesus and allow Him to work as He will. And even if the answer is not what you would have wanted, it's still the right one, and He will provide the strength for you to bear it.

The Canaanite woman came to Him in faith. She asked for the crumbs that might fall from His table. You can do the same. Lay your concerns at His feet. Then, expect a banquet of blessings, but be willing to settle for crumbs.

Come to Me, all you who labor and are heavy laden, and I will give you rest.

~Matthew 11:28.

Chapter Nineteen

ON THE MOUNT OF TRANSFIGURATION WITH JESUS
Transforming with God's Blessing

Reading: Matthew 17:1-9

Jesus spent a lot of time on high mountains. When people traveled from Galilee to Jerusalem, the Bible says they went up, even though the Holy City is to the south. Jesus often went to the Mount of Olives early in the morning to pray. He was on a high mountain when Satan showed Him the kingdoms of the world as part of a three-fold temptation. He was on a high mountain when He pronounced the Beatitudes. And He visited several high mountains to preach and to teach the multitudes that followed Him.

It's no surprise then, that today He has gone to another high place—Mount Hermon, a 9,000-foot, snow-capped mountain in the northeastern part of Israel. Nearby is the city of Caesarea Philippi, which Herod the Great's son Philip established.

Not far away to the east are the ten cities of the Decapolis. Their scattered locations provided an alliance of protection against invaders from the far east.

The surrounding territory is home to a vast heathen population, mostly Greeks who have built temples to their false gods.

How appropriate that, only six days ago, Jesus was in this heathen location asking His disciples who they thought He was. How amazing that Peter would know the answer. "You are the Christ, the Son of the living God," he said, distinguishing Jesus as the One True God, dispelling the false gods and idol worship that prevails in this very place.

You catch sight of the mountain, speechless as you take in the awesome majesty of the towering slope. As you draw nearer, you pass through a field of wheat, then a fruitful valley, bordered by flourishing greenery. The area is fed daily by the icy water that flows down from the mountain's snowy crown. Luscious vegetation springs up all around, sending the sweet scent of fresh flowers into the air. Iridescent butterflies flit among the red thistles and orange speckled buds. White flowering clematis blends with the variegated shrubbery in multiple shades of browns and greens. The path is strewn with moss and lichen, creating a soft cushion under your feet.

A cool breeze flows down from Hermon's snow-covered peak. A stream spills down one side and passes through an ethereal blanket of fog on its way to the Jordan.

Jesus and His three disciples, Peter, James, and John, have already gone halfway up the slope where the mountain has leveled off slightly.

You hurry to catch up with them. Only one week ago, Jesus hinted at His approaching suffering, death, and resurrection, which left His disciples depressed and confused.

Now, the three chosen ones have gathered with Him on the side of the hill. Without warning, His face begins to shine like the sun and His robe turns so white it's nearly blinding. Two other figures appear, one on either side of Him. The apostles recognize them as Moses and Elijah. Stunned to silence, the three look on with awe.

Peter is the first to speak. He offers to build three tabernacles, one for Jesus and one for each of the other two. Suddenly, a bright cloud descends upon them, and a voice declares, "This is my beloved Son, in whom I am well pleased. Hear Him!" It's the same voice you heard when Jesus was baptized in the Jordan. Trembling, the three disciples fall on their faces. Overcome, you press your forehead against the cold, hard ground.

When you raise up again, only Jesus stands on the mount. Moses and Elijah have vanished. Jesus charges His disciples to tell no one about what they have witnessed until after the Son of Man has risen from the dead.

Again, the disciples are perplexed, but Jesus eases their concerns with a brief discourse about Elijah's return and the death of John the Baptist, harbingers, He insists, of His own suffering and death.

You descend the mountain, still pondering what you've just observed. The incident not only transfigured Jesus, but it also transformed His followers. From the time we're born, we climb mountains and descend into valleys. We pass through periods of sin and periods of repentance, trouble and deliverance, losses and blessings, but always He is there to help transform our circumstances and our lives in the process.

Reflect now on your current state and decide what in your life needs to change? What flaws or errors or mistaken thinking needs to go through a transformation that only Jesus can accomplish? Examine your relationship with others, both favorable and unfavorable. Are there areas of unforgiveness? Are there unmet needs? Broken relationships? Offer your personal imperfections on your own *Mount of Transfiguration*, and then enjoy the transformation and the blessings that follow.

Therefore, if anyone is in Christ, he is a new creation; old things have passed away; behold, all things have become new.
~2 Corinthians 5:17

Chapter Twenty

AT THE POOL OF SILOAM WITH JESUS
Thirsting for Living Water

Reading: John 7:37-44

It's the Feast of Tabernacles, and, along with many other celebrants, you hurry into the Holy City for the observance. It's one of three major feasts that require the Jews to come to Jerusalem from all parts of Israel and beyond. During this week-long celebration of the harvest, people have erected tents on the hillside, on rooftops, and everywhere possible in observance of Israel's forty-year journey in the wilderness.

Processions move through the city almost continuously. People wave palm branches, citron, and *lulabs*—branches of myrtle and willow tied together with palm fronds. As they pass by, you catch their joyous singing, marvel at their colorful attire, join in their shouts of praise and thanks to Almighty God. People fast, pray, and bring sacrifices to the temple. It's a joyous event.

Nighttime is most memorable. Four huge candelabra cast a glow over the temple, and throughout the evening, celebrants dance around the temple courts bearing torches. The Levites chant from the *thankful* Psalms with high-pitched flutes accompanying their jubilant voices.

You search for Jesus, but it's difficult to find Him. The last time He was in Jerusalem, the Pharisees and chief priests were threatening to kill Him. This time, He has come there secretly.

Some people believe Jesus' claim to be the Son of God—others question the truth of it. Most know the prophecies, yet they have a difficult time believing those predictions have actually come to pass.

At last, you find the Lord in the Temple, in Solomon's Porch, a large portico on the east side of the temple. Many Jewish leaders and chief priests mingle about, discussing matters of the Law and boasting about their accomplishments. Teachers customarily sit on the steps and share their knowledge with groups that gather there.

Jesus is known to be a rabbi by many. He's talking to a rather large crowd. Great division has arisen among them. Some marvel at Jesus' wisdom and His boldness of speech. Others call Him a deceiver. Someone claims He has a devil. One man declares He is the long-awaited Christ. Someone else insists that no one will recognize the Christ when He comes. A few try to capture Him, but He escapes. Still, the feast continues without incident during the week-long rituals and celebrations.

You walk about the temple courts, trying to catch sight of Jesus again. Just beyond the gate is the Pool of Siloam. You go there now and sit for a while on a stone ledge. The oblong, rock-hewn reservoir stands on the sloping cliff above the Tyropoean Valley. The pool's water supply is replenished by a steady stream flowing through an underground tunnel. Built by King Hezekiah in the 8th century BC, the conduit provided water to the residents of Jerusalem during a siege by the Assyrians. Now it serves not only as sustenance but as a place of refreshment and fellowship.

Because of its proximity to the Temple, the priests come there often, fill their gold pitchers, and pour the water on the altar to the blowing of the shofar and loud singing. The ritual has continued for the past seven days. Now, being the eighth day of the feast, the ritual has ceased. The golden vessels stand empty. The priests are at rest.

It's daytime. The sun is high overhead. You return to the Temple court, and again you seek for Jesus. As before, you find Him with the other teachers in Solomon's Porch. Your lips are dry and your mind drifts to the refreshing pool outside the gate. People have gone there to fill their cups. But, you don't want to leave now that you've found Jesus.

At that moment, He stands to His feet and cries out in a loud voice above the noise of the crowd. "If anyone thirsts, let him come to Me and drink. He who believes in Me, as the Scripture has said, out of his heart will flow rivers of living water."

It's as if He read your mind, as if He knows you're mouth is dry.

His words catch the attention of the others, who pause with their empty cups by the open door.

Instead of offering a small drink that will soothe for only a little while, He's offering an entire river of water—*living water*, He says, that will never dry up. And He explains how to acquire such refreshment for life, simply by believing in Him.

He describes this water as having spiritual significance. He says it brings a promise of the Holy Spirit, who will only come to those who believe.

You've accepted the Father. You've believed in the Son. Now Jesus has offered a third member of the Trinity—The Holy Spirit. He's the comforter, the teacher, the One who will point you to the truth. If you're spiritually thirsty, drink of this Living Water. He is not merely for some. He's for all who believe.

And I will pray the Father, and He will give you another Helper, that He may abide with you forever.

~John 14:16

Chapter Twenty-One

IN THE TEMPLE COURT WITH JESUS
Who Will Cast the First Stone?

Reading: John 8:2-11

Y ou're walking toward the Temple, eager to catch sight of Jesus once again. The magnificent structure looms before you, its large, white stones glistening in the early morning sunrise. The shofar sounds from the pinnacle, and a massive gate opens with a groan. The lintel and side posts are embellished with gold vines, artfully crafted by a skilled workman. Herod spared no expense in rebuilding and enlarging Zerubbabel's temple. This work even exceeded the first Temple, which Solomon built in 1,000 B.C.

You step with bated breath through the entrance into a vast public square. The huge, rectangular area stretches before you. Vendors have set up their tables and people mill about jingling their purses and bargaining with the merchants. This is the Court of the Gentiles. Anyone can enter here. Other courtyards have restricting walls. One designated for Jews only bears a threat of death to anyone else who passes.

You remain in the outer courtyard amidst the rise and fall of voices bartering over vegetables, fresh and dried fruit, herbs and spices, and stacks of fresh baked breads. Fabric sellers unravel colorful swaths of cloth and flap them in the air. Money handlers exchange silver shekels for the distasteful foreign currency brought in by visiting travelers. Merchants sell doves and sheep and cattle for food or for sacrificial offerings. Already a trail of smoke rises from the altar beyond the dividing wall, and the smell of singed flesh fills the air. Farther inside the temple courts, Levites raise their voices in song, like a distant, heavenly chorus.

A vast pavement of multicolored squares stretches before you. Casually, you wander about, pass through the Beautiful Gate into a more serene area of the temple. You expect to find Jesus there, strolling beneath a sheltered arcade or seated on the steps with the teachers of the Law. You find Him sitting amidst the pillars at the bottom of a wide limestone stairway. As usual, a large group of people have gathered around Him and are listening to Him teach.

At that moment, a group of scribes and Pharisees enter the court, their black robes fluttering, their striped shawls swaying with each pronounced step. Before them stumbles a woman whose clothes have been torn and dirtied from the filth of the streets. The officials toss her to the ground before Jesus and accuse her of breaking Moses' Law regarding adultery. They insist the Law calls for her to be stoned. Their hands grip the means of punishment. These are not small stones, but large hunks of jagged rock, heavy enough to end the woman's life.

But something isn't right. First of all, the Law commands that both the man and the woman caught in adultery should face the penalty of stoning. So, where is the man?

What about the other disciplinary options? Such a situation might merely call for "putting away" or divorcing the guilty party.

Finally, such judgments are typically made by the Sanhedrin. Why did these officials bring this woman's judgment before Jesus, unless they mean to entrap Him?

Jesus has faced these men on many occasions. He does not appear to be intimidated now. He rises to His feet, bends over, and writes with His finger on the dusty ground.

The men repeat the challenge. Jesus straightens and boldly confronts them.

"He who is without sin among you, let him throw a stone at her first."

Without waiting for a response, He again bends over and writes on the ground. You cannot see what He has written, but it's made a huge impact on the officials. One by one, beginning with the oldest to the youngest, they drop the stones and leave the court. Jesus is standing alone with the trembling woman, her head bowed in shame.

Of all the men who approached her this morning, Jesus is the only one who can rightfully throw a stone. Instead, He offers mercy. "Woman, where are those accusers of yours? Has no one condemned you?"

"No one, Lord."

"Neither do I condemn you; go and sin no more."

It's easy to identify with the sinful woman, for we all have sinned. But can you also identify with the self-righteous Pharisees and the scribes? After all, haven't we been on both sides of that fence? The question is, would you want to cast the first stone? Very often we don't cast actual stones. We cast hurtful words, and misguided judgments, and destructive gossip. Those are the kinds of stones that hurt most. In order to judge rightfully, sometimes all it takes is to first put yourself in the sinner's shoes.

Judge not, that you be not judged. For with what judgment you judge, you will be judged; and with the measure you use, it will be measured back to you.

~Matthew 7:1-2

Chapter Twenty-Two

AT THE HOME OF MARTHA AND MARY WITH JESUS
Choosing the Better Thing

Reading: Luke 10:38-42

To reach Bethany you need only take a leisurely half-hour jaunt down the hillside from the city of Jerusalem. Travel along the winding path, lined with a rock wall and rows of slender cypress trees, like soldiers guarding the path. Their deep red barks emit an aromatic scent. Lacy myrtle trees also dot the hillside. Patches of scarlet anemones spread away from the trail and blend with a mix of purple and white wild flowers.

The coo of doves and the warble of pigeons punctuate the silence, and you step quietly so as not to disturb the gentle forces of nature. Closer to the village stand groves of many-branched fig trees bearing the last remnants of purple fruit, the reason for the name *Bethany*, meaning "House of Figs."

The peaceful setting prepares you for an afternoon of rest and relaxation at the home of Martha and Mary. Grouped together on the limestone ridge, the stone and mortar houses form a protective compound around a central courtyard. Paved stairways lead to rooftops that nearly join together in an outdoor communal bonding.

This is where Jesus often spends the night when He comes to this part of Palestine. You catch sight of Him now, stooping to enter the low doorway at the home of Martha, Mary, and their brother, Lazarus. You quickly follow Him inside.

Martha, the oldest sibling of the three, is bustling around a well-equipped kitchen. She rushes in and out of the back door, tending the lamb and vegetables in a pot on an outdoor fire pit. Back inside, Martha quickly arranges dried figs and blocks of cheese on a wooden platter. Stacks of unleavened bread are browning on the fireplace hearth. Their warm aroma draws her quickly to the hearth where she piles the bread on a serving platter and rushes it to the table.

Her brow drips of perspiration, wrinkles of stress crease her otherwise innocent face. She's intent on providing a meal for guests, one of the most important social customs of her day, and she does not want to fall short of such an obligation, especially since Jesus has arrived. Her younger brother, Lazarus, is nowhere in sight. And, for the moment, Martha is alone, with only her younger sister, Mary, there to help.

But as soon as Jesus finds a seat, Mary breaks away from the chores and settles at His feet, her face aglow, her sparkling eyes fastened to His face, like she's anticipating another of the Teacher's wonderful messages.

You stand back and observe the interaction, unsure if you should also sit at Jesus' feet or if you should help Martha, who is now frantically darting about the kitchen. She's slamming platters on a raised wooden table and mumbling under her breath.

Finally, she interrupts Jesus' talk and pleads with Him. "Lord, do you not care that my sister has left me to serve alone? Therefore tell her to help me."

Martha has made two mistakes. First, she's accused Jesus of not caring. Of course He cares. He never stops caring.

Second, she has demanded that He get Mary back to work. Martha can't see beyond her anxiety. She doesn't realize that if she, like Mary, would have first made time to sit with Jesus, perhaps the kitchen work would have gone smoother.

Now, she expects Him to show compassion toward her, like He often does when people approach Him with a need. Maybe she's hoping Mary will hear her plea and be convicted, leap to her feet, apologize, and immediately get to work.

But none of those things happen. Mary doesn't budge. She continues to sit with her legs tucked underneath her skirt and her eyes glued to the Master. Nor does Jesus do what Martha has asked.

"Martha, Martha," He says, instead. "You are worried and troubled about many things. But one thing is needed, and Mary has chosen that good part, which will not be taken away from her."

Instantly, the bubbling kettles, the aroma of lamb stew, the warm, toasty scent of fresh bread all fade from your senses, and the very presence of Jesus takes precedence. At that moment, Mary's choice becomes clear. She has turned her back on the activities of the world. Instead of wearing herself out with acts of service, she's allowing Jesus to minister to her.

Now, the question is, which one are you? Martha or Mary? Or a combination of the two?

Sitting at Jesus' feet early in the morning can provide the strength you need for the day's activities. Even the most challenging tasks can seen easier once you've spent time with the Lord. Perhaps being a Mary first will help you to be a better Martha.

But seek first the kingdom of God and His righteousness, and all these things shall be added to you.

~Matthew 6:33

Chapter Twenty-Three

BENEATH THE SYCAMORE TREE WITH JESUS
Making Things Right

Reading: Luke 19:1-10

Today, you're traveling beyond the Jordan to Jericho. The fertile valley is framed on the east by an arid plateau and on the west by a range of mountains nearly 6,000 feet high. The sparkling oasis and lush lowland receive much of their nourishment from the Jordan River and from gentle streams that meander throughout the land.

Is it any wonder this pristine area captured the attention of King Herod the Great, who built a lavish winter palace a couple miles southwest of Jericho? The much frequented resort has several swimming pools, sunken gardens, and courtyards.

The temperature is warmer in this huge desert oasis than it is in Jerusalem. Giant, swaying palm trees provide ample shade along with a healthy supply of juicy dates. Flourishing gardens offer a midday meal of leeks, cucumbers, and freshly hulled grain. Wildflowers in a rainbow of colors blanket the countryside on both sides of the road. A mix of aromas drift with the undulating breath of wind, which carries the spicy scent of the multi-trunked hawthorn tree, the perfume of the white chokeberry blossoms, and the fresh smell of cloves clustered on bushes close to the road.

By this time, hoards of people have crowded onto the path around Jesus. Up ahead, a little man is scrambling up the gnarled limbs of a huge sycamore tree. He settles on a branch and waits for the entourage to pass by. From that height, he can get a bird's-eye view of Jesus in the midst of the crowd. When he spots the Lord, his anxious expression lights up, and a huge grin spreads across his bearded face.

Some of the people know this man well and have begun to yell insults at him. They say he's Zacchaeus, a chief tax collector of the worst kind, often slipping extra fees in his own pocket. Because of his underhanded transactions, he's become a wealthy man who has little concern for the poor and even less concern about his image.

Jesus pauses at the base of the sycamore tree and tells Zacchaeus He wants to stay at his house that very night. Zacchaeus doesn't hesitate. He clambers down the trunk and settles at Jesus' feet. He's at least a head shorter than every other man in the crowd and some women. Then, this sad, unloved little man goes off with Jesus, happily leading the way to his home.

Bursts of complaints rise up from the crowd. Some even utter accusations against Jesus. "He has gone to be a guest with a man who is a sinner."

Their awaited Messiah has chosen to lay his head on a pillow in this publican's house. Jesus is going to eat the man's food and drink his wine. He's going to visit intimately with the evil man, who deserves punishment rather than mercy.

Even the Pharisees in Jerusalem view tax collectors as sinful men and compare them with robbers and adulterers. The job of a tax collector was considered a vile occupation. As a result, tax collectors had few friends outside of their own career.

The people on the path seem to care little that a spiritual regeneration has taken place right before their eyes. One of their own countrymen, a Jewish man who works for the Romans at the house of customs, sought out Jesus with such passion he climbed a tree to get a better view of Him.

Then this corrupt tax collector does an unexpected thing. He vows to give half his goods to the poor and promises to return fourfold to anyone he has cheated. This commitment should have please some of the people.

The man has not only believed in Christ, he wants to make right any wrongs he has done. To Jesus, this is evidence of a converted heart, for He says, "Today salvation has come to this house, because he also is a son of Abraham, for the Son of Man has come to seek and to save that which was lost."

Zacchaeus had to climb a tree to get a look at Jesus. He had to ignore the taunts of the crowd to receive the Lord into his home.

He had to turn from his way of life to make peace with God. He even committed to making restitution to anyone he had cheated, and he vowed to help the poor. Zacchaeus immediately started living out his faith. He's bearing the fruit that comes with salvation. He's showing his faith by his works.

What an example for us to follow. What an opportunity for self-examination. We too have offended someone at one time or another. Perhaps it's time to heal those fractured relationships. Perhaps it's time to pay back what isn't rightfully yours to keep. Perhaps it's time to help the needy. Like Zacchaeus, we can show our faith by our works.

Thus also faith by itself, if it does not have works, is dead. But someone will say, "You have faith, and I have works." Show me your faith without your works, and I will show you my faith by my works.

~James 2:17–18

Chapter Twenty-Four

AT THE TOMB OF LAZARUS WITH JESUS
Do You Believe?

Reading: John 11: 1-127, 38-45

Y ou've been with Jesus in a palm tree-studded paradise on the other side of the Jordan. Word has come that Lazarus, the younger brother of Martha and Mary, has died.

Jesus tarries there for a couple days, apparently with good reason, then He departs for Bethany, though His disciples remind Him of threats against His life in Judea.

The village of Bethany is fifteen miles away on the southeastern slope of the Mount of Olives. The walk takes several hours along a major road paved by the Romans as part of the empire's massive highway system. The smooth covering of stones and mortar make traveling a little easier through the arid landscape.

Your party arrives outside Bethany in the late afternoon. The temperature has dropped to a bitter chill. It's the cusp of spring, only a few weeks before the Passover. Even at this distance, the incessant weeping and wailing at the tomb reaches your ears. Paid mourners have joined the two sisters in their grief. They're pacing along the road near the grave, their shrill pipes and noisy tambourines filling the mournful air.

Some have arrived bearing small sacks of herbs and jars of ointments. The pungent aromas of myrrh and frankincense swirl in the atmosphere, tickle your nose and irritate your eyes.

Martha has arrived, her body shrouded in black, her own soft weeping lost within the deafening lamentations. She lifts her head and stares with reddened eyes at Jesus.

"Lord, if You had been here, my brother would not have died. But even now I know that whatever you ask of God, God will give You."

This, from busy, fretful Martha. Sometime between her harried housekeeping and today, her faith has grown. Had the brevity of her brother's life made the difference? Or did she learn a profound lesson that day when Mary sat at the Lord's feet?

Jesus took four days to arrive here since He first learned Lazarus was sick. Traditionally, the Jews buried their deceased the day they died. Some believed that the person's soul actually hovered within the tomb for three days in hopes of reentering the body. By the fourth day, the soul would have given up and left. This was the fourth day.

Lazarus' body would have begun decomposing. Yet, Martha has expressed a powerful belief in what Jesus could accomplish.

So it's no surprise when Jesus tells Martha her brother will rise again. A flicker of understanding enters Martha's mind.

"I know that he will rise again in the resurrection on the last day," she says.

Jesus then offers a challenge. "I am the resurrection and the life. He who believes in Me, though he may die, he shall live. And whoever lives and believes in Me shall never die. Do you believe this?"

Martha quickly responds. "Yes, Lord, I believe that you are the Christ, the Son of God, who is to come into the world."

After Mary arrives and expresses her own sorrow that Jesus had not been there for her brother, they go to Lazarus' tomb where Jesus is seen weeping. The mourners silence their instruments. The wailers stop wailing. Jesus draws near to the tomb—a rock-hewn cave carved out of the limestone ridge.

Jesus commands the men to roll the stone away from the opening.. Gasps go up in the crowd. Martha speaks what the others are too stunned to say. "Lord, by this time there is a stench, for he has been dead four days."

Jesus' answer cuts to the heart. "Did I not say to you that if you would believe you would see the glory of God?"

Several men approach the cave entrance and struggle to move the cumbersome boulder away from the opening and into a long hand-dug rut.

This simple tomb isn't like those afforded by rulers of their day. There is no elaborate stonework. No embellishments by skilled artisans. It's simply a cave with an initial chamber and a shelf cut out of the wall for the body. When Martha and Mary die, Lazarus' bones will be buried in a hole in the floor to make room for their bodies.

Jesus thanks the Father for answering His prayer. You ponder this. Such faith, to thank God even before the prayer is answered. But when He cries out, "Lazarus, come forth!" He does so with confidence. Jesus isn't merely releasing a friend from the grave, He's revealing the amazing power and glory of the one true God.

You also may know someone who is suffering on a sick bed. Perhaps it's you. Whatever happens, can you say with Martha that you believe Jesus is the Christ, the Son of God? Can you, like Jesus, utter words of gratitude even before your petition is answered? Can you accept the Father's will? True faith goes beyond getting what we want. True faith is not getting what we want and still believing.

And those who know your name will put their trust in You;
For You, Lord, have not forsaken those who seek You.
                                        ~Psalm 9:10

Chapter Twenty-Five

AT THE TRIUMPHAL ENTRY WITH JESUS
Do You See the King?

Reading: Luke 19:29-40

As He usually does when He's in Judea, Jesus has been staying at the home of Martha, Mary, and Lazarus in Bethany. The mysterious, long-awaited *time* He's been speaking about has finally arrived, and He's about to leave for Jerusalem.

It's late in the day, the Sabbath has ended, a priest has blown the shofar at the pinnacle of the Temple announcing the release from the day of rest.

You catch up with the Lord and His disciples as they approach Bethphage, a nearby village also located at the foot of the Mount of Olives to the east of Jerusalem.

While Bethany means "House of Figs," Bethphage means "House of Unripe Figs." Both little villages were named for the grove of fruit-bearing trees growing on the lower hillside. As you stand at the entrance to Bethphage, you look off to the east and spot the ribbon of paved highway leading to Jericho through the distant sun-bleached wilderness. Only recently did you travel that road with Jesus and His disciples, who were heading for Lazarus' tomb.

Now, Jesus pauses outside Bethphage and tells two of His disciples to go into the town and find a young donkey tied there that no one has ever ridden.

"Loose it and bring it here. And if anyone asks you, 'Why are you loosing it?' thus you shall say to him, 'Because the Lord has need of it.'"

Such instructions might sound absurd to some, but this is Jesus talking. The disciples have walked with Him for three years. They've witnessed miracle after miracle. As they've blindly done on other

73

occasions, the two disciples saunter along the dirt path into the city, moving simply by faith and not by human understanding.

Sure enough, moments later they return, towing the colt behind them, amazed that everything happened exactly as Jesus had said.

The two disciples then remove their outer cloaks and lay them over the colt's back. They cautiously assist Jesus in mounting the animal. Then they quickly step aside, as if they fear the colt will buck its rider off. But the animal receives Jesus peacefully. It's as if he's already been broken and trained for carrying a rider.

The animal is likely less than four years old and looks very much like a small horse, though better fed than most. It's brown in color with tufts of black hair in its mane, and it has a gentle, almost sleepy countenance. Nevertheless, as soon as Jesus is on its back, it begins to prance, kicking up tufts of dust and tossing its head, as though the animal itself understands the importance of his mission.

Without needing the slightest nudge or command, the colt proceeds along the cobbled road up the Mount of Olives, down into the Kidron Valley, and then up another hill to the eastern entrance of the Holy City.

Along the way, more of Jesus' followers descend like a wave of the sea upon the travelers. They toss their linen cloaks on the path before the donkey, much like their ancestors did when they showed homage to Jehu as king. Others wave palm branches in an expression of victory. They cry out praises to God, singing, "Blessed is the King who comes in the name of the Lord! Peace in heaven and glory in the highest!"

You're caught up in the exhilaration. "Glory in the highest!" When was the last time you heard a similar exultation? A flash of memory brings back the story the shepherds told you as you journeyed with them to the stable in Bethlehem. They said angels had sung those very words on the night they appeared to them.

Now you're hearing those same words again, this time from an earthly choir, people who've been waiting for the arrival of the Messiah, for a deliverer to rescue them from Roman rule and to restore their nation under God. Little do they know how much more this Savior-King has planned for them.

The mile-long trek weaves aimlessly among clumps of scrub grass, clusters of broken limestone, and chalky rocks, some the size of a man's fist, others as huge as a boulder. With the setting of the sun to the west, a variety of trees cast their shadows on the trail. Most noticeable are the wild almond trees, their aromatic white blossoms catching the last of the daylight. The moment is temporarily spoiled by the bitter odor emitted by the fruit of the black hawthorn trees. The contrast precludes the bittersweet mission the Savior is on, growing even more bitter as His week of passion approaches.

Are you able to join the crowd? Are you able to lay an imaginary cloak before Jesus? Can you wave invisible palm branches? Can you shout, *Glory in the Highest!*? More than that, can you see Jesus as more than a man riding on a donkey? Can you see Him as Savior? Can you see Him as King?

Rejoice greatly, O daughter of Zion! Shout, O daughter of Jerusalem! Behold, your King is coming to you; He is just and having salvation, Lowly, and riding on a donkey, a colt the foal of a donkey.

~Zechariah 9:9

Chapter Twenty-Six

AGAIN WITH MARTHA AND MARY AND JESUS
Precious Ointments

Reading: John 12:1-11

It's six days before the Passover. Martha and Mary are so grateful Jesus raised Lazarus from the grave and returned their brother to them, they are holding a feast in the Lord's honor. As usual, Martha is serving. As is her nature, she's rushing about the kitchen, piling various foods on platters, and setting them on the table.

Some people never learn, right? But, to be fair, Martha is not complaining about Mary not helping. Perhaps she has come to realize that people are different. Some serve with their hands. Some with their pocketbooks. And some with their acts of devotion.

So it is that Mary comes in carrying a cruse of spikenard, a very expensive perfume with a strong aroma. The essence would have been extracted from the sharp spikes on the small shrub bearing deceptively innocent pink blossoms. The moment Mary uncorks the bottle, the intoxicating aroma fills the room, nearly overpowering the savory aromas drifting off the table of food.

In quiet submission, Mary bows before Jesus and pours the perfume on His feet. Then she unpins her hair, lets the locks fall to her shoulders and uses them to wipe His feet clean. The thick oil clings first to Jesus' feet, then to the individual strands of Mary's hair. You wonder if she will wash it out or cherish the aroma for days.

She who loves to sit at Jesus' feet while her sister is working in the kitchen has just done one more act of worship and this in front of her brother Lazarus and Jesus' disciples, who also are in the room. She's even done this in full view of the Jews and Pharisees who are standing outside the house watching and waiting to add one more crime to the growing list they've compiled against Jesus.

The Pharisees are not only watching Jesus. They've come to see

Lazarus, knowing that Jesus raised him from the dead, a miracle that drew many Jews to believe. The chief priests also have been plotting to put Lazarus to death. Mary's bold act of worship may have put her entire family at risk.

But the danger doesn't only lurk outside the home. It's right there in the house. Judas Iscariot openly criticizes Mary's outrageous use of the ointment.

"Why was this fragrant oil not sold for three hundred denarii and given to the poor?"

Being the one who carries the disciples' moneybag, Judas knows one denarius is equal to a day's wages. So, three hundred denarii would cover a person's needs for nearly an entire year. Judas' complaint seems logical at first.

But the Apostle John eyes the man with skepticism. He suspects Judas cares little about the poor but would spend the money on himself if he could get his hands on it. Perhaps, Judas protested in order to cover up his own greed.

It really doesn't matter what anyone thinks or says. What counts is how Jesus feels about what just took place. He quickly defends Mary's actions.

"Let her alone," He says. "She has kept this for the day of my burial."

Another clue. Jesus has been telling His disciples on other occasions that He will be leaving them soon. Don't they know He's been telling them that His death is imminent? In only a few days He will be arrested and crucified. He will be beaten beyond recognition. Soldiers will take spikes and pierce His hands and the very feet that were bathed in Mary's ointment. You have to wonder if the disciples actually have picked up on Jesus' messages.

"For the poor you have with you always," Jesus continues, "but Me you do not have always."

He hasn't implied they need not care about the poor. He has compared the way people care for the poor with how they would treat Him. He wants the gospel message to be given to everyone, including the blind, the lame, *and* the poor.

There are many ways to give to the Lord. Martha is laboring in the kitchen as a way to thank Jesus for bringing her brother home.

Mary has given up a precious ointment she may have been saving for a wedding or some other occasion. The poor widow gave the last of her savings to the temple coffers. The donkey's owner allowed the disciples to use his colt for the Master. These are outward forms of giving, but Jesus has seen the heart in every situation

Judas revealed his greedy heart by complaining about Mary's use of the ointment. The Pharisees standing outside revealed their evil hearts because they came there to spy on Jesus and Lazarus. At the same time, Jesus saw Mary's broken heart.

Though Jesus wants your tithes, your offerings, and your good works toward others, all of that doesn't mean anything, unless you do so with a sincere heart. That's where the giving should begin. Within the heart. Then the outward act will follow.

The sacrifices of God are a broken spirit, A broken and a contrite heart—These, O God, You will not despise.

~Psalm 51:17

Chapter Twenty-Seven

ON THE MOUNT OF OLIVES WITH JESUS
Preparing for the End

Reading: Matthew 24:1-14

Y ou've entered the Kidron Valley. Three separate paths lead upward to a mile-long ridge known as the Mount of Olives. You choose the path that passes beneath the northeast wall of Jerusalem and enters the garden enclosure known as Gethsemane near the northernmost summit.

Various kinds of trees abound on either side of the trail, but a huge olive grove dominates the top. You reach the highest point, a couple hundred feet higher than Zion. From here, you enjoy an unobstructed view of the Holy City and a good portion of the two and a half miles of thick gray wall that encircles the Temple. Eight separate gates stand at various places around the perimeter. The one most visible is called the Golden Gate.

With that magnificent scene as a backdrop, Jesus has settled on a rock and is meeting privately with His disciples. His recent talks about His imminent departure and the destruction of the temple have incited their curiosity. Now they've come with specific questions on their hearts.

"Tell us, when will these things be? And what will be the sign of Your coming and of the end of the age?"

To satisfy their hunger to learn more, Jesus embarks on a lengthy monologue. He speaks about deceivers claiming to be Christ. He predicts wars and rumors of wars, famines, and earthquakes, calling them the beginning of sorrows. He warns about persecution. He speaks of betrayal, false prophets, and iniquity. Yet, He assures His people, as these things multiply and grow worse, there is hope.

"But he who endures to the end shall be saved. And this gospel of the kingdom will be preached in all the world as a witness to all the nations, and then the end will come."

The End? What He shares next brings much concern, for He speaks about a time of Great Tribulation, the darkening of the sun and moon, stars falling to earth, the shaking of the heavens, and, ultimately, the Son of Man coming on the clouds to gather His own.

The sun is beating hard on the hillside, yet Jesus' message has you shivering. Though you've had plenty of time to rest after your long climb to the summit, your heart is beating as though you are still running uphill. A gentle breeze stirs the locks of your hair, yet your forehead and neck are moist with perspiration.

Your gaze falls on the Temple perched on the northeastern ridge of Jerusalem, and you try to imagine the rubble, the fires, the devastation Jesus has said must come. Then you look around at the olive grove. The trees appear healthy. They're filled with white blossoms and the promise of much fruit. Life abides on this mountain. It's hard to imagine death and destruction, to envision an end.

Think about your own life. Your home. Your family. The town where you live. Now picture it all gone. Rubble. Fires. Dead. Jesus' words have struck you to the core.

But He's also given a promise. "He who endures to the end shall be saved."

The disciples are sitting on the ground at His feet, their faces rapt with attention. He describes those who will endure to the end—the faithful servants instead of the unfaithful ones, the wise virgins instead of those who are foolish, the sheep on Jesus' right instead of the goats on His left.

From Jesus' message, you gather that the faithful servant is someone who has ruled his master's possessions well. In truth, what you consider your material possessions actually belong to Him, and you are simply a manager of those resources. Jesus wants you to be a faithful manager.

The wise virgins are those who have acquired oil for their lamps and are ready for the bridegroom's arrival. What is the condition of your spiritual lamp? Have you kept filling the reservoir with the oil of the scriptures? Have you stoked the fire with prayer?

Then there are the sheep on His right side. They will have per-formed many acts of kindness toward others. They fed the hungry, gave drink to the thirsty, took in strangers, and visited the sick and those in prison. Are you among the faithful sheep?

Perplexed, the disciples ask Him when they did all those things.

"Assuredly, I say to you, inasmuch as you did it to one of the least of these, My brethren, you did it to Me."

The least of these. They're all around you. You only have to look for them.

The end is coming. No one knows when. But Jesus has told us what to expect. And He's told us how to be a faithful servant, a wise virgin, and a sheep on His right. Pay attention. Be alert. Use your talents well. The end may be closer than you think.

His Lord said to him, "Well done, good and faithful servant; you were faithful over a few things, I will make you ruler over many things. Enter into the joy of your Lord."

~Matthew 25:21

Chapter Twenty-Eight

IN THE UPPER ROOM WITH JESUS, PART I
Beware of Betrayal

Reading: Matthew 26:20-25

It's the 14th of Nissan, the first day of the week of Unleavened Bread. Jesus has sent Peter and John ahead to prepare the Passover meal in Jerusalem. He tells them to follow a man carrying a pitcher of water into a house and request permission from the owner of the house for use of the upper room. Much like the two who were able to get a donkey for Jesus' entrance into Jerusalem, Peter and John follow the Lord's unusual instructions and are able to find a place.

For centuries, most of the houses in Palestine have had a rooftop shelter where people could sit and enjoy the sunset or simply spend a while in meditation and prayer. Some of those rooftop settings were constructed with huge canopies that sheltered guests who spent the night or gathered for dinner and conversation there.

The more expensive homes, like the one you're entering now, have a large enclosed area on the roof with four walls, windows and a roof of its own. The furnishings are elaborate—ornate tapestries to block out harsh weather, golden candlesticks to light the room, plush pillows and thick, woven mats for reclining, and a wooden table for serving food and drink.

To reach the upper room, you mount an outer stair, constructed of lengths of wood cut from Lebanese cedar trees and fitted together close to the wall of the house with a waist-high railing to prevent falls. At the top you pass through an open door into a well-lit room, and the scent of cedar stairs gives way to the soothing aroma of olive oil warming on bowls held by the candlesticks.

The homeowner has provided a one-year-old lamb, dressed and roasted outdoors on a spit and now resting on a large platter in the center of the table. Other pieces of fine pottery contain bitter herbs, in remembrance of the slavery the Israelites endured in Egypt, unleavened bread to signify the haste with which they escaped their captivity, and a mixture of apples, dried fruit, and nuts, like the mortar the enslaved Israelites used to construct Pharaoh's buildings. Each place at the table has four cups of wine and a bowl of salted water relating to the tears the Israelites once shed.

Jesus is sitting at the head of the table, and the twelve are seated around the other three sides. You squeeze in between two of them, thrilled to be included in their Passover meal, yet sadly aware that this is the last time the disciples will dine with their Master.

At the conclusion of the blessing, conversations rise up around the table. You watch the others and follow the rituals of the meal, first dipping a sprig of parsley in the salted water, then following with a portion of the fruit. There are no table utensils. Like the others, you tug a piece of lamb from the bone, then you bite into the crispy outer shell and savor the juicy meat inside. You lift a piece of unleavened bread from the platter, tear it in half and bite into its warm crust. You use the other half to soak up the rich broth from a bowl in the center of the table.

Conversations are interrupted when Jesus makes a statement that leaves everyone in shock. "One of you shall betray me," He says.

Then, one-by-one, with trembling voices, they each ask the question that could bring condemnation or release. "Lord, is it I?"

"He who dipped his hand with me in the dish will betray me."

All eyes turn toward Judas Iscariot. His hand is hovering over the bowl of broth, a sopping piece of bread between his fingers.

"Rabbi, is it I?" he asks weakly.

Jesus nods. "You have said it."

It's hard to believe one of the twelve will betray the Master. Judas walked with Jesus for three years. He witnessed the miracles, heard the discourses and the parables. But somewhere along the way he turned against the Lord. Somehow, Judas forgot, or maybe he never really believed in the first place. Now he's arranged to hand Jesus over to the chief priests for a mere thirty pieces of silver, a month's wages, and according to the prophet Zechariah, the value of a slave. Judas has placed a disgustingly low value on the life of the Son of God.

Sadly, it can be that easy to fall into Satan's trap. It happens when we stop believing Jesus is who He claimed to be. We may condemn Judas for his betrayal, but we also have a little bit of Judas inside us, for we were born with the same sinful nature. The main thing is to keep the betrayer in check. You must fight to remain faithful. Fight to keep watch over your soul. Fight to stay loyal to the One who bought you with His life.

Stand therefore, having girded your waist with truth, having put on the breastplate of righteousness, and having shod your feet with the preparation of the gospel of peace, above all, taking the shield of faith with which you'll be able to quench all the fiery darts of the wicked one. And take the helmet of salvation, and the sword of the spirit, which is the word of God.

~Ephesians 6:14-17

Chapter Twenty-Nine

IN THE UPPER ROOM WITH JESUS, PART II
Keep Remembering

Reading: Matthew 26:26-29 and Luke 22:19

Nighttime is falling. The apostles light more candles. A golden glow bathes the faces around the table. Judas has left the upper room. Only eleven apostles remain.

Many diverse personalities fill this room. John, the son of Zebedee, may be the youngest one there. Like a child, he's moved closer to Jesus and is resting his head on the Lord's breast. Your heart swells. What deep love this disciple must have for the Savior. And how Jesus must also love him.

John's brother James is nearby. The two have been known to raise dissension among the others at times, and have earned the title *Sons of Thunder*. A short time ago, they even had their mother request places of honor on either side of Jesus in the coming kingdom. Such a mix of personalities, yet they remain faithful to the Master.

Then there's Peter, an impulsive, outspoken man. During the meal, he adamantly declares he will never deny Jesus. Then he also refuses to allow the Lord to wash his feet, but quickly changes his mind when Jesus tells him he can have no part with Him, at which time Peter offers his whole body to be washed. That's Peter. From one extreme to another.

Near the end of the meal, the Lord takes the flat, round bread, says a blessing over it, and breaks it in pieces which He distributes around the table. This is traditionally done at Passover meals with the host saying, "This is the bread of the affliction which our fathers ate in the land of Egypt." But, Jesus doesn't say the customary recitation. Instead, His next remark leaves the apostles momentarily stunned.

"Take, eat, this is My body."

You remember another time when He associated His body with bread. Specifically, He'd declared He was the *Bread of Life*, which immediately incited the Jews, giving them one more reason to kill Him.

This time, however, no one questions Jesus' statement. Not even Peter. They simply consume what He has offered them and continue to give Him their attention. He then takes a cup, gives thanks, and passes it around the table for each one to take a sip.

"Drink from it, all of you. For this is My blood of the new covenant, which is shed for many for the remission of sins."

Once again, He speaks about heaven, as though He's planning to leave them soon. By now, they've heard His predictions. He's told them He must suffer and die. Now here He is, comparing bread to His body and the dark red wine to His blood. He's predicted what is about to befall Him, but they still don't get it.

You've read the scriptures. You already know about Jesus' arrest, His trials, His crucifixion, burial, resurrection, and ascension. You'd love to share what you know with the disciples, but you're just a fly on the wall, a silent phantom in a chair at the table.

Very soon, they also will know the truth. The mystery will unravel before their eyes, and then they will understand the significance of the bread and the wine.

At the beginning of the feast, the disciples followed tradition and sang a portion of the Hallel, taken from Psalms 113 and 114. Now, they pick up the remaining portion as they prepare to leave the upper room singing Psalms 115 to 118. They're on their way to the Mount of Olives, the very place where Jesus likes to end His days when in Judea.

You follow them along the cobbled path through the Golden Gate on the eastern side of the city wall. Still singing, the disciples march ahead, their steps light, their shoulders back, their heads turning from left to right, like a group of happy celebrants, caught up in the Passover's remembrance of the Israelites' release from bondage.

After crossing the Kidron Valley, you reach the Garden of Gethsemane on the western slope of the Mount of Olives. From there, you can look back at the sprawling Temple complex and the giant wall wrapping its protective arms around the city. Jerusalem rests on the distant hills where ancient sarcophagi mingle with family tombs carved out of the limestone ridges.

Within the garden, old olive trees line both sides of the trail, their gnarled trunks and deformed limbs creating eerie shadows over the landscape. Through the cluster of blue-green leaves you view a blanket of stars overhead.

The dark of night is settling on the mount, yet the experience in the upper room continues to echo in your mind. You recall Jesus' final words after He shared the bread and wine. "Do this in remembrance of Me." Such a strange request, yet it seems important to the Savior. Perhaps by occasionally repeating the breaking of bread and the sipping of wine, you'll always appreciate Jesus' sacrificial gift to those who believe.

You are my God, and I will praise you; You are my God, I will exalt You. Oh, give thanks to the Lord, for He is good! For His mercy endures forever.

~Psalm 118:28-29

Chapter Thirty

IN THE GARDEN WITH JESUS
Staying Awake

Reading: Matthew 26:36-46

Y ou've crossed the Kidron Valley and have entered the Garden of Gethsemane near the base of the Mount of Olives. A stream of water runs from the temple into the valley, carrying with it the blood of hundreds of sheep being sacrificed at the altar. Though the red-stained brook meanders close to the garden, a bitter-sweet atmosphere prevails in the sheltered cove where a proliferation of olive trees, some of them hundreds of years old, block out the noise of the city.

You walk along the rock-lined path among several olive presses constructed of large stones mixed with rubble. The presses are silent now, but in a few weeks they'll come to life. Workers will shake the branches of the olive trees, causing the fruit to fall like thousands of raindrops to the hard ground. They'll gather them up and take their baskets to one of the presses where a laborer will guide a beast of burden around the circular press, pulling a big, round stone over the olives, separating the pits and extracting the rich oil into a pan lying underneath.

This is Gethsemane, which means *Olive Press*, and it's the place Jesus has chosen for his final moments of freedom.

As the sun disappears beyond the wall of the Holy City, the trees cast full shadows over the garden. In the stillness of night, your senses come alive with the sounds of crickets in the brush and nighthawks circling overhead.

No one else is here except for the eleven who have come with their Master. At Jesus' command, they sit together on a grassy mound. Their stomachs are full. They're tired. And they just completed a two-mile walk from Jerusalem. While in the upper room, they listened to Jesus speak about the present life and a future home with many mansions. He prayed aloud for them. He spoke about the coming of the Holy Spirit, a new concept for the disciples, for they can expect guidance, teaching, and comfort from this unseen visitor from heaven.

Now relaxing in the garden, they're surprised when Jesus leaves them sitting there and singles out three—Peter, James, and John—to a separate area. You follow them. Jesus tells them to watch and pray. Deeply distressed, He then goes off a little way, falls on His face, and prays aloud.

"O My Father, if it is possible, let this cup pass from Me, nevertheless, not as I will, but as You will." You marvel at the dichotomy of such a prayer. Jesus has expressed His desire, yet He's willing to let it go in favor of the Father's will.

Then He returns to the three disciples and finds them asleep.

"What? Could you not watch with Me one hour?" He says, obviously grieved. "Watch and pray, lest you enter into temptation. The spirit indeed is willing, but the flesh is weak."

But, as soon as Jesus walks away, the three drop off to sleep again.

Two more times, Jesus repeats His plea to the Father, and two more times, He says, "Your will be done."

Standing at a distance, you've been given the privilege of watching Jesus' struggle between His humanity and His deity. As a human, He very likely had head colds, foot sores, stomach distress, and toothaches. He faced temptation, but He never sinned.

As God in the flesh, He healed others of similar maladies and more. He spoke about a heavenly kingdom. He knew what His enemies were thinking. And He managed to avoid capture. Until tonight.

The human part of Him is agonizing over what He, as God, knows is about to take place. Each time, He's uttered those same four self-condemning words. "Your will be done." Though troubled and fearful, He's submitting to the Father's will. The only thing He asked of the apostles was that they should stay awake and pray with Him.

I hate to admit it, but there are times I've "fallen asleep" to the needs of others when I should have been alert and praying. Perhaps you've also fallen asleep when your prayers and comfort are needed most. Looking back, do you wish you had said something? Or done something?

More opportunities will come. People will call on you for your help, for a kind word, or for prayer. One day, your own well-being might depend on your staying awake and praying. Let the experience in the garden train you for such a moment.

Like Jesus said, "Watch and pray, lest you enter into temptation. The spirit indeed is willing, but the flesh is weak."

Be sober, be vigilant, because your adversary the devil walks about like a roaring lion, seeking whom he may devour.
~1 Peter 5:8

Chapter Thirty-One

AT THE HOME OF CAIAPHAS WITH JESUS
Have You Denied Him?

Reading: Matthew 26: 57-75

You stand in shock as Judas Iscariot, originally one of the twelve, presents Jesus to the authorities with a kiss on the cheek. The traitor's hand holds tightly to the thirty pieces of silver he received for the betrayal.

A band of the chief priests' soldiers, armed with swords and torches, lead Jesus out of the garden and down the hill into the valley. You follow, your heart breaking with every crunch of the stones beneath your feet.

The entire party then begins a steady climb along the ridge past the caves and tombs to the mount of Jerusalem. Ahead is the broad stone wall encircling the city, and beyond, the Temple, Herod's palace, and the home of Caiaphas, the high priest, like a huge masonry complex strung together in the Upper City. The soldiers push Jesus through the Sheep Gate, like a lamb being led to slaughter, for this is the very gate the shepherds use when bringing their sacrificial animals to the temple.

Inside, the way is paved with broad, marble slabs, smooth and cool beneath your feet. You pass the pool of Bethesda and follow the meandering road into the housing district. Huge courtyards loom on either side. Their tan walls nearly disappear behind flowering vines, their blossoms closed in sleep during the night. Large metal gates open to quiet gardens where long shadows have fallen upon dormant vegetable plots, marble statues, and fountains within the courtyards of the wealthy.

The darkening sky has brought a deceptively peaceful mood to Jerusalem. Bats dart noiselessly overhead. An owl releases a mournful wail somewhere in the trees. Except for the soft scraping of your sandals on the pavement, the world is still. It's as if all of nature has sensed the onset of a bitter-sweet event.

The armed guard leads Jesus, bound and shackled, into Caiaphas' residence below the Temple complex. As the high priest, Caiaphas serves as president of the Great Council, the Sanhedrin, which consists of seventy additional influential men of the city. Many members of this group have been plotting to kill Jesus since the day He raised Lazarus from the grave. Now Caiaphas is about to hear the charges.

Like most others, you are relegated to a broad courtyard paved with flagstones and surrounded by two-story buildings. The doors of several great halls open up to the outer court. Angry voices pour from one of those halls as the chief priests present their evidence at an informal hearing, which is quickly followed by a mockery of a trial—the scramble for witnesses, the false testimonies, Jesus' soft-spoken claim to be the Son of Man, Caiaphas' harsh rending of his robe, and then the guilty verdict, followed by a series of vicious attacks, with men brutally punching and slapping Jesus, spitting in His face, and daring Him to prophesy who had struck Him.

By this time, you're trembling beside Peter and John. You look around the crowd that has gathered. None of the other disciples are there, and with good reason. If the authorities can so easily attack Jesus, what will they do to His followers?

Then a servant girl recognizes Peter and remarks that he was with Jesus of Galilee. He quickly denies the charge and moves on to another porch within the complex. Puzzled by Peter's response, you follow him. Here's the interminably outspoken Peter, the bravest of the disciples, shrinking under the accusation of a mere maid.

Another girl recognizes him as one of Jesus' followers, and, cursing, he again denies the accusation. You shake your head. This was a man who not very long ago called Jesus "the Christ, the Son of the living God." What has become of such great faith?

More people come along and insist that Peter was one of Jesus' followers. With more cursing and swearing, Peter denies ever knowing the Man. With each denial, Peter's countenance grows more and more regretful.

It's near the break of dawn. Immediately the crow of a rooster sails over the rooftops, and Peter is reminded of Jesus' prediction that before the rooster should crow, Peter would deny Him three times.

Deny Jesus? *Never.* Yet, Peter did so, and he did it openly. He quickly leaves the courtyard, weeping bitterly.

If a man like Peter could deny Christ, then how can any of us declare we never would? Other questions surface. Does denial happen only with a spoken word? Or do we deny Christ in other ways? Like when we fail to listen to a prompting of the heart to tell someone about His most precious gift. Or when we allow our lives to blend in with the world, making one excuse after another . What about when we fail to take a stand for righteousness, or when we refuse to defend the gospel?

Denial can take many forms. Sometimes we simply need to be bold, suppress our fears and embarrassment, and trust Jesus with the outcome.

Watch, stand fast in the faith, be brave, be strong.
~1 Corinthians 16:13

Chapter Thirty-Two

IN PILATE'S COURT WITH JESUS
What is Truth?

Reading: John 18:28-40

The night is gone. The rooster has crowed. Battered and accused of crimes against the government, Jesus is now being led to the Praetorium, the Roman governor's official residence in Judea. The arresting party reaches a broad stretch of colored flagstone known as the Pavement, the place of judgment over those who have committed crimes against Rome. Many windows and doors open to the Pavement from high on the outer wall. They lead to the great halls of judgment.

So, it seems, the charge of blasphemy before the Sanhedrin only a few hours ago has now been changed to one of political offense. Jesus will now be judged by Marcus Pontius Pilate, who was awarded the governorship of Judea in AD 26.

From the frowning crowd of people, voices speak of their growing dislike for this man. In the few years of his rule in Judea, Pilate stirs up an atmosphere of dissent whenever he comes to the Holy City.

"Why didn't he stay in Caesarea," mumbles one man. "What is he doing in Jerusalem?"

"Don't you know?" says his companion. "It's the Passover. Pilate comes here for all of the Jewish feasts. He knows that when the city is overrun with visitors, there's more likelihood of insurrection."

"He's a liar," remarks another, cursing. "He pretends to favor the Jewish people, but he can't be trusted. He's quick-tempered, stubborn, and he wavers from one side to the other, trying to please everyone, but in the end, pleasing no one."

"He acts like he's above us all, but he came from the middle class," another man sneers. "His rise to power came about only because of his military skills. He's used his power for evil. Only last week he allowed his soldiers to bring idols into the city."

"Yes, and now he has the power to pass a verdict on Jesus," someone else says. He points toward the Hall of Judgment, a raised platform with a window overlooking the pavement. Pilate has settled on a *bema seat*, a three-legged wooden chair with a high back, the final place of authority. After interviewing Jesus, the governor declares Him to be innocent of any civil crime. He wants to send Him back to the Jewish authorities. But the Jews adamantly refuse to try Him. They insist Jesus is guilty of a political crime and claim they do not have the authority to put Him to death.

The Jewish officials refuse to step one foot inside the Praetorium for fear of being defiled by entering a place of the Gentiles and be forbidden to partake of the Passover. But you can enter the Praetorium. You pass through the open door and stand in the shadows. At that moment, Pilate asks Jesus if He is the King of the Jews.

"My kingdom is not of this world," Jesus replies.

Pilate continues to press Him. "Are you a king then?"

Jesus doesn't falter. He admits that He is a king. Not a Roman king, but a king who came into the world to bear witness to the truth. He's implied that He came from outside the world—from heaven, in fact.

Pilate seems to miss the point. "What is truth?" he says.

Little does Pilate know, the Truth is standing directly in front of him.

Without waiting for Jesus to answer, Pilate once again finds no fault in Him. The man has tried everything within his power to free Jesus. But the crowd in the courtyard has grown even more vocal. Pilate sees little recourse than to offer to release one prisoner in honor of the Passover. Jesus? Or a violent insurrectionist named Barabbas?

When the crowd calls for the release of Barabbas, Pilate relents and hands Jesus over to his soldiers to be scourged. They plait a crown of thorns and press it against Jesus' brow, drawing blood. They place a purple robe around His shoulders, and once again they mock Him for His claim to royalty, and they punch Him in the face.

Jesus is led away to be crucified, one of the most horrific forms of capital punishment devised by the Romans. As He goes, you recall Pilate's question during the interrogation. "What is truth?"

Very often, the world's idea of truth conflicts with what the Bible says. The world is changing and getting farther away from God. But God's word never changes. It's time we not only seek the truth but also defend it. The truth can lead us to make the right choices. For instance, which group of people would you have joined? Knowing what you know now, you would call for Jesus' release. But what if you hadn't read the scriptures? What if you had been born in that day and time? Is it possible you would have joined the crowd that called for the release of Barabbas?

You can still choose. Will you pick Jesus? Or Barabbas? Jesus? Or the world? Jesus? Or false comfort. So many choices, but only one right answer.

And you shall know the truth, and the truth shall make you free.

~John 8:32

Chapter Thirty-Three

ON GOLGOTHA WITH JESUS
Forgiving Your Enemies

Reading: Luke 23:32-43

With a heavy heart, you follow Jesus along the cobbled road to Golgotha, which means *a place of a skull* in the Aramaic language, named thus because the barren knoll had the shape of a human skull. Also known as Calvary in the Latin, the place of execution is located outside the city wall on one of the main roads leading into Jerusalem, making the suffering visible to multitudes who travel in and out of the city.

Jesus stumbles along the path ahead of you. The purple robe has been removed from His back, exposing His torn and battered flesh. As was their custom, the Roman soldiers carried out His punishment flailing many strands of leather embedded with bits of glass and sharp nails. Even though Simon of Cyrene is bearing the heavy crossbar for Jesus, the brutality of the soldiers has nearly finished Him.

At Golgotha, Jesus endures even more cruelty. The Roman soldiers pound thick nails into His wrists and heavy iron spikes into His feet. The loud ring of the hammer against the nails resounds amidst the anguished cries of those being crucified. Jesus' executioners then attach the crossbar to the post. Under Pilate's orders, they fasten a sign over His head, *This is the King of the Jews*, written in Greek, Latin, and Hebrew. The three languages represent the diverse gathering at the foot of the cross, a poignant message to every nation and tribe of the world. Then, their muscles straining under the weight, the soldiers raise Jesus' cross and thrust it into a deep hole where it holds fast.

Jesus' adversaries continue to mock Him. The Roman soldiers have begun dividing His clothes among themselves. The indifferent look on with curiosity or pass by unaffected by the brutality, for such punishment has become common since the Roman invasion.

Then there are Jesus' followers. They've either blended in with the crowd or they're standing far off, helpless to do anything. Only John, the young fisherman, stands at the foot of the cross, along with Mary, the mother of Jesus, and three other women. It's no wonder Jesus places the care of His mother in the hands of this beloved disciple.

From the cross, Jesus looks down with sadness at the angry crowd, shaking their fists and screaming curses at Him, some even challenging Him to come down.

Then He speaks. "Father, forgive them, for they do not know what they do."

You're standing so close you breathe the smell of dirt mixed with blood, you hear the moans of the two men who have been crucified on either side of the Lord. You weep with Jesus' mother. You wish you could pull down that cross and remove the nails.

Then you consider what has happened here today. Jesus has asked the Father to forgive His persecutors. He's demonstrated that very act of forgiveness in a brief conversation with the criminals on either side of Him.

One of them is mocking Jesus and daring Him to save Himself and them too. But the other defends Jesus' innocence and admits his own sin. Then he turns to Jesus. "Lord, remember me when you come into Your kingdom."

Jesus responds. "Today you will be with Me in Paradise."

You stand in awe. Even as He hung there suffering, Jesus not only begged forgiveness for the people in the crowd, He extended it to a known criminal. The poor man didn't have to come down off the cross. He didn't have time to run around Jerusalem doing good deeds. He didn't even have time to be baptized. This man's salvation depended only on one thing—his admission of guilt and repentance.

It's twelve o'clock noon, a time of day when the sun usually beats down on the city. But the sky has grown dark and remains in darkness until three o'clock in the afternoon. At that time, the earth quakes beneath your feet. Rocks fall from a nearby cliff. People panic. The ground opens up. Then, Jesus cries out with a loud voice, "Father, into Your hands I commit my spirit."

You witnessed first-hand what your Savior endured for mankind. You heard the false evidence. You cringed during His scourging. You shook your head over the crowd's accusations drowning out His followers' pleas for mercy. You saw this as defeat, but Jesus has claimed victory. He's bound our sins to His cross. Something truly life-changing has happened here today.

Even in death Jesus has set an example for us to follow. In the midst of His suffering, He forgave His enemies. But what about you? Have you found it difficult to forgive someone? Whether the individual has apologized, like the thief on the cross, or if that person has behaved like the Jewish authorities, condemning you, or like the Roman officials, attacking with vengeance, you also can forgive. This is unconditional forgiveness. Just as Jesus has extended it to you, you also can extend it to your adversary.

And be kind to one another, tenderhearted, forgiving one another, even as God in Christ forgave you.

~Ephesians 4:32

Chapter Thirty-Four

AT THE EMPTY TOMB WITH JESUS
Because He Lives

Reading: Mark 16:1-11 and John 20:11-18

Three days have passed since Joseph of Arimathea and Nicode-mus, two prominent Pharisees, asked Pilate for Jesus' body and quickly made arrangements to bury Him in Joseph's family tomb, because the Law called for immediate burial after death.

Nicodemus came to the cross carrying an alabaster jar filled with a mix of aromatic spices and myrrh. The woody, bitter-sweet fragrances went between the folds and strips of linen of Jesus' burial cloths. This they did quickly, racing against time, because the Sab-bath was about to begin.

Now here it is, Sunday morning, and you're approaching the garden tomb, a short distance from the city's Damascus Gate and not far from Golgotha, the place of the crucifixion. The surrounding landscape takes your breath away, for this is one of the more elite locations for burial in Judea. This is the place where the wealthy bury their loved ones, where Joseph himself expects to be interred one day.

The area is lush with vegetation. Streams of light break through the branches of myrtle trees. Towering cedars cast their scent into the air. Giant palm trees spread their lacy umbrellas overhead. Nearby olive trees shower the lawn with white blossoms. Flowers in all shades of the rainbow lift their faces to the rising sun. There are no briars or thorns here. Only a radiant garden that speaks of life instead of burial and death.

You tiptoe over the stone walkway toward the tomb, shocked to find the stone has been rolled away. A stairway constructed of stone slabs leads down to the entrance and beyond. It's a true rich man's tomb, ornately decorated with scrollwork carved into the stones.

At that moment, several women come up behind you. One of them is Mary Magdalene, the woman Jesus freed of seven devils. The others are Mary, the mother of James the Less and his brother Joseph. Then there's Joanna, the wife of Chuza who works in Herod Antipas' palace, and Salome, the wife of Zebedee and mother of James and John. All of them have faithfully followed Jesus during His three-year ministry.

Now they've come here carrying vials of sweet spices. The aromas blend with the scent of the awakening flowers beside the path. You step aside and let the women pass, for they've come to anoint Jesus' body.

But the ground trembles beneath their feet, and they stop short of the entrance, frowning in puzzlement. They too notice that the stone has been rolled away into a ditch, leaving the cave open. Cautiously, they step inside. You follow them into the darkness. Sunlight filters through the open door revealing a large chamber, about six feet long, nine feet wide, and ten feet high. Many niches and shelves have been carved out of the wall, most likely for members of Joseph's family. Beyond is a second chamber reserved for the final burial after the mourning period has ended.

The tomb hadn't been used until now. It's completely empty. Even Jesus' body is gone. Only His grave clothes lie neatly arranged on the slab where Joseph had lain Him.

As your eyes adjust to the shadows, you see a young man, clothed in white and sitting on the burial ledge. Startled, the women gasp and grab each others' hands.

"Do not be alarmed," the man says. "You seek Jesus of Nazareth, who was crucified. He is risen! He is not here. See the place where they laid Him." Then, he tells the women to go to the disciples and let them know that Jesus will meet them in Galilee.

Filled with excitement, the women rush off. You watch them go, then you turn around and find the shimmering young man also has vanished. You're standing in an empty tomb, alone and pondering what has just happened. You emerge, still dazed, into the blinding sunlight, and discover Mary Magdalene has returned to the open tomb. She's sobbing with heart-rending grief.

She believes someone took Jesus' body away during the night and laid Him somewhere else. But there He is, standing right in front of her, though she does not recognize Him.

Then, He speaks her name. "Mary!"

He tells her He has yet to ascend to the Father and instructs her to go and tell the disciples what she has seen. Obediently, and with newfound joy, she hurries off to share the good news.

You also know what that good news means. Jesus has defeated death. He's been resurrected, the first of many, as He promised. This miraculous event should give hope to all who have trusted in Him. It proves He is who He claimed to be. His resurrection has declared that the grave will not be our final resting place. There truly is life after death.

O Death, where is your sting? O Hades, where is your victory? The sting of death is sin, and the strength of sin is the Law. But thanks be to God, Who gives us the victory through our Lord Jesus Christ.

~1 Corinthians 15:55-57

Chapter Thirty-Five

ON THE ROAD TO EMMAUS WITH JESUS
Burning Hearts

Reading: Luke 24:13-35

It's the afternoon of Jesus' resurrection. Now that you know His plan, you start off for Galilee, in hopes of beating the disciples there. The women have told them they could meet Jesus near the sea. Not only that, but with the Passover ended, they can return home.

Along the way, you encounter two of Jesus' followers who are going to Emmaus, a little more than seven miles northwest of Jerusalem. Because it lies in the general direction of Galilee, you expect to find rest there during your journey.

The two men are wearing traveling clothes—short tunics for easy movement, veils to block the sun's blistering rays, sandals thicker than the ones they wear for leisure. They're carrying goatskins, likely filled with water, evidenced by the moisture that has gathered on the outside. As they walk, one of them named Cleopas is dining on a handful of figs. The other man has bitten into a piece of unleavened bread.

The road is taking them away from the arid mountainous region near Jerusalem and closer to the lush Valley of Aijalon, where cactus grows to the height of a man, and cedar and fruit trees abound. The dirt path is packed hard having survived the pounding of many feet over the centuries. All is still except for the sudden stirring of air rustling the withered grass on either side of the path.

It was here in the Valley of Aijalon that God honored Joshua's prayer more than 1,200 years before Jesus came and caused the sun to stand still for one day, long enough for the Israelites to thwart the attack of the Amorites.

But the two men walking along this ancient trail are not conversing about Joshua's victory. Nor are they speaking about where they expect to stay in Emmaus and their plans for the next day. They're talking about what happened in Jerusalem over the weekend. With noticeable sadness, the two are remembering the crucifixion and burial of Jesus and the disappearance of His body from the grave.

Suddenly, out of nowhere, Jesus has drawn near to the two men. He steps in stride with them the way any traveler might do when joining others. Like Mary Magdalene, they don't recognize Him. Instead, their voices rise with indignation as they fret over having lost the only person who might have saved the Jews from Roman oppression.

Then, with their new companion prompting them, they talk about Mary's visit at the tomb and the report she gave the disciples. Then, beginning with Moses and the prophets, Jesus expounds on the scriptures, particularly those that speak of His coming. His corrective but encouraging discourse continues until you reach Emmaus. Soothed by His words, the two men plead with Jesus to come in and eat supper with them.

Like you've done many times before, you sit unseen at their table. You recline on a woven mat with a plump pillow behind your back. The table is laden with bowls of fresh fruit, platters of bread, and slivers of lamb, along with pitchers of red wine.

It isn't until Jesus breaks the bread and hands them each a piece, that the two men's eyes are opened and they realize who has been talking to them. No sooner are they filled with unspeakable joy than He vanishes.

One of them says, "Did not our heart burn within us, while He talked with us on the road, and while He opened the Scriptures to us?"

Jesus has likely gone off to Galilee, as He had promised. The two men, however, decide to return to Jerusalem, eager to share their experience with the eleven. Since it's late in the day, you decide to spend the night in Emmaus and then leave for Galilee in the morning. You lay on a bed of straw, gaze out a window at the darkening sky, and consider the significance of the prophecies Jesus had mentioned.

Isaiah had spoken about a virgin miraculously conceiving and giving birth. The prophet also wrote about a Wonderful Counselor, Mighty God, Everlasting Father, Prince of Peace. Micah spoke of Bethlehem as the Savior's birthplace. Zechariah wrote about the deliverer arriving in Jerusalem on the back of a donkey. And the Psalms are filled with allusions to Jesus' crucifixion.

When you read the Old Testament prophecies, do you view them as mere historical data and nothing more? Do they serve only as bits of trivia to be shared at your next Bible study gathering? Or, like the two men on the road to Emmaus, does your heart burn within you as you consider their significance? The two men hurried back to Jerusalem to share the news. You have opportunities to do the same in your realm of life. At such times, those you speak to might also feel that burning within the heart.

Do not think that I came to destroy the Law or the Prophets. I did not come to destroy but to fulfill.

~Matthew 5:17

Chapter Thirty-Six

BEHIND CLOSED DOORS WITH JESUS
The Disease of Doubting

Reading: John 20:19-29

Following a promise that Jesus would be meeting with them, the disciples have gone to Galilee and have gathered behind closed doors.

After spending the night in Emmaus, you also go there with great expectation. You approach the house, a two-story structure constructed of blocks of stone smoothed over with swaths of mortar. A huge iron gate opens to a large courtyard. A wooden staircase travels upward hugging the side of the house. You climb to the rooftop enclosure, then pause before a wooden door, it's panels milled from aromatic cedar. Two stone posts and a broad lintel create a sturdy frame for the door. You knock gently and listen for the padding of bare feet. Dark eyes peer through the opening. You state your purpose, that you've come as a friend, and the door opens wide enough to let you pass.

You look around the room, a spacious area, suitable for large gatherings. Only ten of the disciples have come. With the traitor now deceased, eleven should be here. You count again. Only ten. Then you mentally go through the names.

There's Peter and his brother, Andrew. James and John, the sons of Zebedee. There's Nathaniel, Philip, Simon the Zealot, Bartholomew, Matthew, and Jude. So, where is Thomas?

No one seems to know. He should have been invited to the gathering. The disciples regularly meet these days, but always in secret since the Lord's crucifixion, which left them confused and fearful. So why isn't Thomas here, dining with the others, talking about the recent sightings of the Lord? The first report given to them by Mary Magdalene and the other women was followed by an excited account by the two men who were traveling to Emmaus. Still, they're not sure they believe the tales.

The ten are squatting on mats around a long, low table where food already has been laid out. You lower yourself to a mat between two of the fishermen. The aroma of seared fish fills the air. A large platter piled high with the day's catch is in the center of the table along with a bowl of honeycombs and a basket of unleavened bread. You're about to reach for a piece when a familiar voice causes you to freeze.

"Peace to you." Jesus is standing in their midst. Unlike the walk to Emmaus, He didn't stroll into the room. He simply appeared!

The disciples tremble, for their Jewish faith has instilled in them concerns about the spirits of the dead coming back to life.

But Jesus immediately offers comforting words. He shows them His hands and His feet, still bearing the marks of the crucifixion. He invites them to touch, proving that He is flesh and bone and not a spirit at all.

If that isn't enough proof, he receives a piece of the broiled fish and a honeycomb, and he sits down to eat with them. No dead man can do what He is doing. Neither can the spirits of the dead.

He continues to minister to them with enlightening words about His purpose, citing the scriptures that predicted His suffering, death, and resurrection. Before leaving, He gives them the promise of the Holy Spirit.

Jesus' leaves, Thomas arrives. The disciples tell him they have seen the Lord. But he eyes them with skepticism. "Unless I see in His hands the print of the nails, and put my finger into the print of the nails, and put my hand into His side, I will not believe."

The ten shake their heads with disgust. There's no convincing a man who first needs to see in order to believe. You finish your meal and depart.

Eight days later they're together again in the upper room. This time Thomas is with them. Like before, the doors are shut. No one can come in unless one of the eleven opens the door. Suddenly, Jesus is standing in their midst. He says, "Peace to you!" Then He turns to Thomas. "Reach your finger here, and look at My hands, and reach your hand here, and put it into My side. Do not be unbelieving, but believing."

Thomas exclaims, "My Lord and my God!" The doubter has declared the truth. Jesus truly is Lord and God. You look to Jesus for His response.

He says, "Thomas, because you have seen Me, you have believed. Blessed are those who have not seen and yet have believed."

Seeing is believing. You've heard the expression many times in the past. But it has no place here or anywhere else when the Lord asks us to believe.

Now answer this. Are you like Thomas? Do you need to see to believe? Or can you believe without seeing? That's the beginning of really trusting God.

Now faith is the substance of things hoped for, the evidence of things not seen. For by it the elders obtained a good testimony.
~Hebrews 11:1-2

Chapter Thirty-Seven

ON THE SHORE OF TIBERIUS WITH JESUS
Do You Love Him?

Reading: John 21:2-17

You're standing on the western shore of Tiberius. The pear-shaped expanse stretches as far as the eye can see. Also known as Galilee, it's the largest freshwater lake in Israel, extending thirteen miles from north to south and more than seven miles from east to west. At some places, particularly in the north, the lake is up to 200 feet deep.

Mountain terrains embrace the sea on both sides, with the hills of Galilee on the west near the place where you are standing, and the cliffs of the Golan Heights embracing the shore on the east side. It's springtime now, and the slopes are green with life. Later in the year, they'll turn brown as the vegetation dies off and the mountain peaks—particularly Mount Herman in the north—will turn white with snow.

For now, you can enjoy the breeze poring off the lake bringing with it the scent of freshwater fish. And you can bask in the warmth of an early morning sunrise.

The beginning rays cast long, golden streaks across the water. The disciples have been fishing all night, as is their habit. Peter and six other disciples have gone back to their old job. They're coming now, their sails billowing, their vessels tacking from left to right as they draw closer to the shore. Then, the fishermen lower their sails and man their oars for the last few yards, dragging their empty nets behind them.

Jesus is standing on the shore waiting for them to arrive. Once again, He commands another casting of the nets, this time to the right side of the boat. Though not yet aware it's Jesus, they obey, and moments later, they're dragging heavily laden nets behind them. They gaze at the shore and realize it has to be Jesus.

Jesus has already started a fire on the shore and is roasting several pieces of fish over the coals. The early morning cookout emits the crackle of tiny flames and the pungent aroma of blackened fish.

"Bring some of the fish which you have just caught," Jesus calls out to His disciples. "Come and eat breakfast."

Peter is the first to respond. He's already waist deep in the water, having plunged into the sea when he saw the Lord. After dragging his net to shore, he counts his load—153 very large fish—yet his net has not broken.

This is the third time Jesus has shown Himself to His disciples since His resurrection. Thomas no longer doubts the truth. They all agree Jesus has risen from the grave. What's more, He's not only alive, He's eating and drinking with them.

You settle on a stretch of sand littered with pebbles and sea shells. Peter hands you one of the seared fish. You sink your teeth into the outer crust and savor the tender meat inside, leaving only a skeleton to be tossed into the fire. You follow with a wedge of soft, warm bread. Food has rarely tasted as good as what you are now enjoying as you squat before an open fire at the edge of the sea, early in the morning, with Jesus and the disciples by your side.

At the end of the meal, Jesus takes Peter aside and asks him three times if he loves Him. Only a couple weeks ago, Peter denied Jesus three times. Perhaps Jesus is giving His disciple a chance to make up for his failure. Instead of using the name Peter, which means "rock," Jesus has reverted back to the man's pre-salvation title, Simon, which means "pebble," and He includes the appellation, "son of Jonah." So Peter is once again a fisher of fish—not of men—and the child of a fisherman.

"Simon, son of Jonah, do you love Me more than these?" Jesus asks three times.

And each time, Peter's response is the same. "Yes, Lord, You know that I love you."

"Feed My lambs," Jesus says. Then, "Feed My sheep," He says two times.

Though their discourse uses two different Greek words for the word *love*, the overall message is clear. Does Peter love Jesus enough to care for His sheep? His three admissions of love seem to have canceled his three denials from only a few days ago. But the question remains, does he love Jesus enough to once again become a fisher of men?

What about you? Do you love the Savior enough to put aside your feelings of insecurity and reach out to the lost? Do you love Him enough to ignore your own wants, needs, and material desires in order to help others? Will you stash the pearl of great price in a drawer, or will you tell someone how to get one too? Will you store your treasures in a new barn, or will you share some of your wealth with those in need?

Loving Jesus is more than simply saying you do. Such a commitment involves action. It involves loving others. So the question remains: Do you love Him?

You shall love the Lord your God with all your heart, with all your soul, and with all your mind. This is the first and great commandment. And the second is like it: You shall love your neighbor as yourself.

~Matthew 22:37-39

Chapter Thirty-Eight

ON A HIGH MOUNTAIN WITH JESUS
Go Therefore

Reading: Matthew 28:16-20

Jesus has summoned His disciples to Mount Arbel, a high mountain on the west side of the Sea of Galilee. Without hesitation you hurry there, aware that the Lord has something important to say. At 1,200 feet above sea level, it's the tallest mountain in the region and offers a wide view of the landscape.

You approach this huge mass of barren elevation, and it's difficult to believe eleven men are going to climb its rugged side. A strong wind off the lake could very well stir up a whirlwind of blinding sand. Nevertheless, Jesus is waiting there on a ridge, and the disciples are already making their way upward along a shear cliff to a level spot about a third of the way up the mountain.

You step ahead with confidence. If they can climb this trail so can you. The struggle takes your breath away, but you persevere, knowing He's there on the slope. Finally, you stand on the ridge and turn to gaze at the sparkling blue water below. From this height the Sea of Galilee seems to lose its power. It appears tranquil now, a serene body of water with sailboats like toys floating lazily on its surface.

To Jesus' faithful followers, a host of memories surround this place. The shore below brings to mind the day when Jesus called Peter and the others to become fishers of men. In the distance stands Magdala, the home of Mary whom Jesus healed of seven devils. Also a prosperous fishing village, Magdala is home to one of the oldest synagogues in the region. Also nearby is Cana, the tiny village where Jesus performed His first miracle by turning water into wine at the wedding of friends.

The eastern side of the mountain plummets precariously into a basin, where a vast number of natural caves once served as shelters from invading forces but now remain empty. Other high places include the Golan Heights and the snow-capped peak of Mount Hermon. It was in this region, near the city of Caesarea Philippi, that, in response to Jesus' question, Peter declared, "You are the Christ, the Son of the living God."

With all of these memories swirling around in their heads, the disciples have made it to the ledge where Jesus is standing. They gather around their Master and fall before Him in worship. You also drop to the hard ground, with little concern for the sharp pebbles that pierce your tired knees. The moment Jesus begins to speak, a hush falls over the eleven. They settle back on the hard ground, their eyes fastened on their teacher, their hearts clinging to every word.

"All authority is given to Me in heaven and on earth," He tells them, and then He presents a challenge.

"Go therefore and make disciples of all the nations, baptizing them in the name of the Father, and of the Son, and of the Holy Spirit, teaching them to observe all things that I have commanded you: and lo, I am with you always, even to the end of the age."

Once again, Jesus has promised to always be with them. They're confused because He's already told them He must leave so the Holy Spirit can come and abide with them. They are to teach all nations. Teach them what? They are to baptize, but not the way John the Baptist did. This baptism will involve the Holy Spirit.

Jesus has sent out His followers before—two by two, carrying a small bag, wearing only one coat. Seventy of them went door to door and from town to town, remaining where they were welcomed and moving on while shaking the dust off their feet when rejected.

The eleven don't yet know how to obey Jesus' final edict, but you know, because you've read the Book. Though they're confused now, after Jesus has ascended into heaven, they will gather in each other's homes. They will pray and talk about all that Jesus taught them while He was with them. And they will consider more seriously the Great Commission He has entrusted to them here on this high mountain.

And not to them only. It's time you and I began to take Jesus' challenge seriously, for He gave it to all of His followers, not just to the eleven. He said the fields are ripe and ready for harvest. The fields of the world are far too expansive for eleven men to handle.

You eye the disciples with intense respect. Some will head out and reap a harvest on foreign soil. Some will touch multiple souls in their own country, in their own regions, in their own neighborhoods. Some will make a difference in their own homes.

The Great Commission has not changed over the centuries. It wasn't only meant for the eleven, but also for you. Have you planted any seeds? Has your crop been watered? Are the buds blooming? Has the fruit appeared? Does more work need to be done? Most importantly of all, are you up to the task?

He who continually goes forth weeping, Bearing seed for sowing, Shall doubtless come again with rejoicing, Bringing his sheaves with him.

~Psalm 126:6

Chapter Thirty-Nine

AT THE ASCENSION OF JESUS
Be Witnesses Wherever You Are

Reading: Acts 1:6-11

Forty days have passed since Jesus rose from the grave. During that time He visited often with His disciples, and He appeared to more than 500 of His followers.

Now He's summoned His disciples to the Mount of Olives, at 2,600 feet one of the highest hills in Judea. The hilly ridge runs for two miles from north to south along the eastern side of Jerusalem. From here, you can enjoy a magnificent view of the Holy City and the Temple. Below, a winding road weaves through the wilderness to Jericho fifteen miles away, where the barren landscape gives way to a brilliant green oasis.

A sense of foreboding prevails today, for this could very well be the last time the disciples see their Lord. You take a long, last look at the setting. A chalky limestone floor mixed with rust-colored clay lies beneath your feet. A lush olive grove covers the western slope down to the valley with its ancient tombs and proliferation of wild almond and black hawthorn trees.

Many of the Lord's followers—men, women, and children—have joined this gathering. Such an assemblage can only mean one thing. Jesus is about to depart.

He stands on the knoll and surveys His people. The conversations die down. You catch your breath as He begins to speak.

First, He tells the crowd to remain in Jerusalem and wait for the baptism of the Holy Spirit. He's promised this member of the Godhead before in recent days. But the disciples appear to be more concerned about the future of their nation.

"Lord, will You at this time restore the kingdom to Israel?"

Nothing would please the disciples more than to be rid of the

Romans. But that isn't why Jesus came to earth. Though He's mentioned His purpose multiple times, they still don't understand. Jesus came to save the lost.

With amazing patience He overlooks their ignorance and repeats His promise to send the Holy Spirit after His departure. Then He lays a new burden upon them.

"You shall be witnesses to Me in Jerusalem, and in all Judea and Samaria, and to the end of the earth."

He has repeated the Great Commission and has named actual locations where their ministry will take place. Jerusalem, where they relocated since leaving their homes in Galilee. Judea, an even broader area. Samaria, the land of Gentiles. And ultimately, the end of the earth, many locations where none of them have ever been.

While they are still pondering His message, Jesus is taken up into a cloud and disappears from sight. Your heart pounds with the realization that you have witnessed first-hand the ascension of the Lord into heaven.

All faces are turned upward. All eyes are on the wisp of clouds overhead. Then, two men in glowing white garments appear on the mount with a final promise. "Men of Galilee, why do you stand gazing up into heaven? This same Jesus, who was taken up from you into heaven, will so come in like manner as you saw Him go into heaven."

Jesus left mere seconds ago, and these men have already mentioned His return. You shift your gaze from the sky to the ground. This very place where you are standing will one day welcome Him back.

The Mount of Olives stands to the east of Jerusalem. Jesus will come from the east, just as He already has told His followers, "For as the lightning comes from the east, and flashes to the west, so also will the coming of the Son of Man be."

Like a bolt of lightning, His return will happen fast and with blinding radiance.

Your heart beats stronger. Your breath comes faster. And you know. The departing message Jesus gave to His disciples He also gave to you. Go into all the world, He said. Beginning with Jerusalem.

The Holy City was not the disciples' hometown. Most of them

came from the region of Galilee. Nevertheless, Jesus' commission had them focusing first on Jerusalem, the place where they often gathered for festivals and much of their early ministry. Then farther out in Judea, then even farther, Samaria.

So where is your Jerusalem? Where is your Judea? Your Samaria?

We all know missionaries who have traveled to the uttermost parts of the earth. Yet, not all of us are able to go. Instead, we reach out to people within our immediate surroundings. Aside from that, we support those who go beyond the borders. We pray. We provide financial help. We send care packages. Everybody's mission field is personal and different. Yet, ultimately, we will all share in the harvest.

So then neither he who plants is anything, nor he who waters, but God who gives the increase.

~1 Corinthians 3:7

Chapter Forty

ON THE ISLE OF PATMOS WITH JESUS
Faithful in the Midst of Persecution

Reading: Revelation 1:9-20

You're entering the Isle of Patmos during John the Apostle's time of exile. Once an ancient flourishing acropolis with many magnificent buildings and fortresses, you now find it a rock-infested wasteland under Roman control. This is where some prisoners come during their time of punishment. The Emperor Domitian exiled John here, along with Prochurous, his amanuensis, or secretary.

To say it is a wasteland is an understatement. Gone are the Greek markets and the well-groomed homesteads. Gone are the prolific gardens. Gone is the fishing industry. And gone are the shrines to the Greek goddess Artemis.

The Patmos of John's exile is a lonely, desolate place, a volcanic island now riddled with large hunks of chalk-white granite and small, black obsidian stones. Except for patches of colorful wild-flowers, vegetation is sparse, and only a few trees bear citrus, walnuts, and figs. The ground consists of brown clay dusted over with sand that swirls like mini-tornadoes with the slightest breath of wind.

Patmos is ten miles long and six miles wide, a small slice of earth within a group of islands in the Aegean Sea. Your boat docks inside a cove in the middle of the seahorse shaped island. You step ashore and immediately begin your search for John. Soon, you find him perched on a cliff overlooking the azure sea below. A grove of feathery tamarisk trees cast shadows on the hillside. The air is crisp and clean, bearing only the slightest taste of the sea.

John doesn't complain about the damp cave where he's found shelter from the elements or the rock he uses for a pillow at night. A fisherman by trade, he lives off the sea and whatever he can forage within the sparse vegetation. Though in his late 90s, John is not concerned about his lonely estate. He has plenty of writing materials and a secretary to record his messages.

You watch from a distance and take care not to disturb the apostle's time of contemplation. Suddenly, John straightens, for he's been startled by a voice. To you, it's merely the wind whistling among the rocks. But then, you sense another presence, and though you only see the rough and weathered landscape, someone has definitely entered this place of seclusion.

A loud voice breaks the silence claiming to be the Alpha and Omega, the First and the Last. The same voice tells John he must write down what he will see and send the report to seven specific churches in Asia.

Another breeze stirs up the warm, luxurious aroma of oil burning. Before John are seven, tall, golden lampstands, and standing in their midst, One like the Son of Man. His ankle-length garment is bound at the chest by a gold belt. His pure white hair speaks of wisdom rather than age. The fire in His eyes pierces your very soul, and His sandals shine like polished brass. He's holding a rod with seven stars and from His mouth comes the image of a two-edged sword.

You've been given a great gift seeing the vision John will write about. The aura is so intense you cannot deny God's presence.

Overcome, John falls to the ground and presses his forehead against the hard, cold earth. Humbled beyond words, you also drop to your knees and then prostrate on the ground, unable to raise your face. Gradually, the aura dissipates, and you sense the withdrawal of the heavenly presence.

The voice then gives more instructions meant only for John. Immediately, the apostle rises from the ground and hurries off, calling for Prochurous. The two stride together toward their cave. You follow them and move from piercing sunlight into a dark, damp recess in the rock wall. Prochurous lights a candle and leads the way, down, down, down, to the bottom of the cave, then to a far corner where he assumes his place at a stone table. It's a small space with a ceiling that brushes against the top of your head. Prochurous unravels a parchment, lifts a stylus, and awaits John's instructions.

Undaunted by the persecution he endured at the hands of the Roman emperor, John dictates this recent experience. You watch the battered apostle with interest, for rumor has it he was boiled in oil but survived without a scar on him, and you wonder how much more punishment will he receive because of his association with the Savior.

We don't have to be exiled to Patmos to face persecution. Ill treatment will come in many forms, in your hometown, your workplace, your school, or anywhere you endure opposition to your faith. Will you, like John, keep going no matter what happens? Will you face the attacks confident that the Lord will carry you through it? You can expect His intervention when needed. He is only a prayer away.

Trust in the Lord with all your heart, And lean not on your own understanding; In all your ways acknowledge Him, And He shall direct your paths.

~Proverbs 3:5-6

Chapter Forty-One

BEFORE THE HEAVENLY THRONE WITH JESUS
Behold the King

Reading: Revelation 4:1-11

Want to feel small and insignificant? Come now to God's heavenly throne. Does it match what your limited human understanding imagined it would be like? Probably not.

Man typically thinks of God's throne as a big chair with plush padding, maybe some gold trim, and a halo around it. Doubtful. God's throne has to be far greater than that. Heaven itself is bound to be far greater than anything we see on earth.

Get ready for a profound revelation. First of all, you've been invited to heaven by the loud blast of a trumpet. Like John, you're speechless. You're probably trembling. And, you're feeling very much like a little child.

Again, a loud voice like a blaring trumpet has summoned you before God. Now behold! Our Lord is sitting on His throne. He's exchanged the crown of thorns for a royal, magnificently jeweled crown. He's exchanged Pilate's purple robe for a shining garment. His once pierced hands now hold a scepter. His once mutilated feet wear sandals of burnished brass.

The throne itself is engulfed in glorious brilliance with many sparkling stones—bright red jasper, deep brown sardine, and the shimmering green emeralds. You're standing on a sea of glass so pure it looks like crystal, deceptively fragile, yet it bears the weight of the throne. Seated on twenty-four thrones arranged on either side of the Lord's throne, are twenty-four elders. They're clothed in brilliant white robes, and they have glittering gold crowns on their heads.

You're paralyzed, unable to speak or move. Lightning bolts crash all around the throne. There is no delay for the thunder, for it occurs spontaneously with each flash of brilliance. Seven lamps emit flames of fire before God's throne. And four beasts have taken different forms, each of them with six wings and many eyes that seem to look everywhere. The feeling of being watched takes your breath away. You can't move. You can't speak.

Nor has John spoken or budged in the least. He's simply taking it all in, recording everything in his mind, perhaps, with plans to record it all on another piece of parchment.

Then the most profound worship takes place. The four beasts have begun to sing, "Holy, holy, holy, Lord God Almighty, who was, and is, and is to come."

The overwhelming spirit of worship consumes you, and when the twenty-four elders fall down before the One on the throne, you're swept along with their zeal. They cast their crowns before the throne. You also bow down, but you have no crowns to cast. You have yet to win the Imperishable Crown for faithful endurance, the Crown of Rejoicing, for those who rejoice in difficult times; the Crown of Righteousness, which can never be earned for it's based on Christ's righteousness and not our own; the Crown of Glory, given to those who love His appearing, and the Crown of Life, for being faithful even unto death.

Someday, you'll have crowns to cast. For now, you can only watch the elders remove theirs and place them at Jesus' feet. But you can join the chorus. You can sing praises along with the others.

You are worthy, O Lord,

To receive glory and honor and power,

For you created all things,

And by Your will they exist and were created.

As though in a dream, you continue to stand in awe as the One on the throne lifts a sealed book. But no one is worthy to break the seal, except the Lamb who was slain.

More revelations unveil before you. For the moment, you have stepped away from the tangible, finite things of the earth, and you have entered another realm, one that seems like a fantasy but is even more real and lasting than the tangible.

The truth is, reading about all these things in the scriptures should make just as much of an impact on you as experiencing it all beside John. You don't have to see the vision to understand what a great and powerful God sits on the throne in heaven.

A trip through the book of Revelation should produce the same level of wonder as you would experience if you were actually called up to heaven as a witness. Read the book and let your imagination soar. The details of each chapter should prepare you for what is to come. Though much symbolism is woven through the passages, and the descriptions sometimes seem vague, the overall message is clear. The end is coming.

Don't wait for heaven to worship the One on the throne. You can join the chorus right now. In your church. With a community choir. In the privacy of your own bedroom or, like some of us, in our personal echo chamber called a shower.

Just remember, worship doesn't begin and end at the heavenly throne. It begins in your heart, and it ends in the heart of God.

Oh come, let us worship and bow down; Let us kneel before the Lord our Maker.

~Psalm 95:6

Conclusion

You've gone back 2,000 years without having stepped inside a time machine. You've traveled across the sea without having purchased an airline ticket. And you've gotten a deeper sense of Jesus' teachings through His words and actions during His time on earth.

This journey's purpose wasn't for entertainment reasons. Nor was it meant to be a rewrite of the Bible. The preceding chapters should merely have drawn you closer to God through the lessons Jesus taught and the examples He demonstrated.

It's my hope that the vivid descriptions helped place you directly in the midst of things as they happened back then. Hopefully, you saw more than just a mountain that looked like every other mountain, a temple greater than any modern-day architect could hope to design, a body of water with a startling, bipolar personality.

As you return to the present, hang onto the images. Let them serve as a springboard as you continue to delve into the scriptures. Look beyond the printed word and envision the time and place, the people, the colors and sounds, the aromas and sensations of that period in time. Travel with Jesus into the past where you can learn from Him, and then return to the present where you can put those lessons into practice. Then, ultimately, you should look forward to the future where lies your eternal hope.

May you be richly blessed.
Marian Rizzo

Those who go down to the sea in ships,
Who do business on great waters,
They see the works of the Lord,
And His wonders in the deep.
For He commands and raises the stormy wind,
Which lifts up the waves of the sea.
They mount up to the heavens,
They go down again to the depths;
Their soul melts because of trouble.
They reel to and fro, and stagger like a drunken man,
And are at their wits' end.
Then they cry out to the Lord in their trouble,
And He brings them out of their distresses.
He calms the storm,
So that its waves are still.
Then they are glad because they are quiet;
So He guides them to their desired haven.
Oh, that men would give thanks to the Lord for His goodness,
And for His wonderful works to the children of men!
Let them exalt Him also in the assembly of the people,
And praise Him in the company of the elders.

Acknowledgements

Many thanks to my beta readers—Paul Ferguson, a dear friend and fellow writer; Marge Forrest, owner of Gabriel's Christian Book & Supply in Ocala, Florida; The Rev. Donald J. Curran, rector at Christ the King Anglican Church of Ocala, and Joanna Jones, my daughter and faithful confidante.

With much appreciation I want to recognize my editor/publisher, Mike Parker of WordCrafts Press. He truly has demonstrated the patience of Job while working with this temperamental, perfectionist writer, all the while guiding my work to a worthwhile finish. Also, many kudos go to David Warren, one of the best cover designers in the business.

I also appreciate my writer friends with the Ocala chapter of Word Weavers International. Their critiques and words of encouragement have proven an invaluable resource as I stumble ahead with each new manuscript.

Ultimately, the most heartfelt praises have to go to Jesus Christ, my Lord and Savior, the guide and finisher of my work and life. As He has promised, He has never left or forsaken me.

Bible Almanac, The; Ed. by James I. Packer, Merrill C. Tenney, William White Jr.; Guideposts, Carmel, New York; Thomas Nelson, Nashville, 1980.

Everyone in the Bible; William P. Barker; Fleming H. Revell Co., Westwood, NJ., 1966.

Great People of the Bible and How They Lived, Reader's Digest Assoc., Pleasantville, NY, 1971.

Harper's Bible Dictionary, Madeleine S. Miller and J. Lane Miller; Harper & Row Publishers, New York, 1973.

Josephus, Complete Works, Translated by William Whiston, A.M.; Kregel Publications, Grand Rapids, Mich., 1981

King James Study Bible, The; Thomas Nelson, Nashville; Liberty University, 2013.

New Chronological Bible, The; KJV, Ed. by R. Jerome Boone; World Bible Publishers, E.E. Gaddy & Assoc., 1980.

New Unger's Bible Dictionary; Merrill F. Unger; Ed. R. K. Harrison; Contributing Editors, Howard F. Vos and Cyril J. Barber; Moody Bible Institute, Chicago, 1988.

Roget's Super Thesaurus; Marc McCutcheon; Writer's Digest Books, Cincinnati, 1995

Plus, multiple online references, virtual tours, and an actual visit to the Holy Land.

About the Author

A Pulitzer Prize nominee in the field of journalism, Marian Rizzo has won numerous awards, including the New York Times Chairman's Award and first place in the 2014 Amy Foundation Writing Awards. She worked for the *Ocala Star-Banner* newspaper for 30 years. She also has written articles for the *Ocala Gazette*, *Ocala Style Magazine*, and Billy Graham's *Decision Magazine*.

Several of Marian's novels have won awards at Florida Christian Writers Association conferences and Word Weavers International retreats. In 2018, her suspense novel, *Muldovah,* was a finalist in the Genesis competition at the American Christian Fiction Writers Conference. Two of her novels earned Amazon Best Seller status. Through her membership with Word Weavers International, she's been able to hone her craft through interaction with other members and critique sessions.

Marian earned a bachelor's degree in Bible education from Luther Rice Seminary. She trained for jungle missions with New Tribes (now ETHNOS 360), and she served for two semesters at a Youth With A Mission training center in Southern Spain. She also served as a field and telephone counselor at the Billy Graham Crusade in Boston in 1982 and at Franklin Graham's Festival in Gainesville, Florida, in 2002.

An in-person tour of the Holy Land provided much of the backdrop for her biblical era books, and helpful information came from numerous virtual tours and online research.

Marian lives in Ocala, Florida, with her special needs daughter, Vicki. Her other daughter, Joanna, has blessed her with three wonderful grandchildren.

Also Available From

WordCrafts Press

SonShine: Reflections of Faith
Beverly Clopton

Illuminations
Paula K. Parker & Tracy H. Sugg

Pro-Verb Ponderings
Rodney Boyd

Devotions from Everyday Jobs
Tammy Chandler

I Wish Someone Had Told Me
Barbie Loflin

www.WordCrafts.net

www.ingramcontent.com/pod-product-compliance
Lightning Source LLC
Chambersburg PA
CBHW031421120626
46545CB00006B/2210